THE
ORGANIZED
KITCHEN

Keep Your Kitchen Clean, Organized, and Full of Good Food—
and Save Time, Money, (and Your Sanity) Every Day!

Brette Sember

Aadamsmedia

Avon, Massachusetts

Published by
Adams Media, a division of F+W Media, Inc.
57 Littlefield Street, Avon, MA 02322. U.S.A.
www.adamsmedia.com

ISBN 10: 1-4405-3056-4
ISBN 13: 978-1-4405-3056-2
eISBN 10: 1-4405-3262-1
eISBN 13: 978-1-4405-3262-7

Contains material adapted and abridged from *365 Ways to Live Green* by Diane Gow McDilda, copyright © 2008 by F+W Media Inc., ISBN 10: 1-5986-9808-7, ISBN 13: 978-1-5986-9808-4; *The Everything® Classic Recipes Cookbook* by Lynette Rohrer Shirk, copyright © 2008 by F+W Media Inc., ISBN 10: 1-5933-7690-1, ISBN 13: 978-1-5933-7690-1; *The Everything® Green Living Book* by Diane Gow McDilda, copyright © 2007 by F+W Media Inc., ISBN 10: 1-5986-9425-1, ISBN 13: 978-1-5986-9425-3; *The Everything® Home Storage Solutions Book* by Iyna Bort Caruso, copyright © 2006 by F+W Media, Inc., ISBN 10: 1-5933-7662-6, ISBN 13: 978-1-5933-7662-8; *The Everything® Meals for a Month Cookbook* by Linda Larsen copyright © 2005 by F+W Media Inc., ISBN 10: 1-5933-7323-6, ISBN-13: 978-1-5933-7323-8; *The Everything® Organize Your Home Book* by Jason R. Rich, copyright © 2002 by F+W Media Inc., ISBN 10: 1-5806-2617-3 ISBN 13: 978-1-5806-2617-0, *The Everything® Freezer Meals Cookbook* by Candace Anderson, copyright © 2010 F+W Media, Inc., ISBN 10: 1-4405-0612-4, ISBN 13: 978-1-4405-0612-3.

Printed in the United States of America.

10   9   8   7   6   5   4   3   2   1

Library of Congress Cataloging-in-Publication Data
is available from the publisher.

This book is available at quantity discounts for bulk purchases.
For information, please call 1-800-289-0963.

Contents

Introduction

The kitchen is one of the most used rooms in the entire house. Americans do (almost!) everything there. In many homes it is the primary gathering area. Asking one room to do so much can lead to disorganization and chaos. If you've ever experienced the frustration that comes from not being able to find what you need when you need it, this book is for you! It's a complete guide that will help you take charge of your kitchen. Not only will you learn useful tips and strategies for finally tackling the clutter and craziness that exists on your counters and behind all of your cupboard doors, you'll also discover ways to organize *how* you do things in the kitchen. The end result? An organized kitchen that meets your needs.

In Part 1, you'll learn how to take back your kitchen:

- Chapter 1 shows you how getting your kitchen under control can benefit everyone in your family and offers some quick tips to get you going.
- Chapter 2 takes a look at how to bring energy and harmony into your kitchen through techniques like feng shui as well as how to imbue the room with your personality.
- Chapter 3 discusses how to manage and organize all the other (non-cooking) activities that are a part of kitchen life.

In Part 2, you'll learn the nitty-gritty details of getting—and keeping—your kitchen organized:

- Chapter 4 discusses what equipment you most need in your kitchen with tips on how to organize and store it.
- Chapter 5 delves into drawers and cupboards, and with lots of helpful suggestions and ideas, helps you purge, reorganize, and restructure how you're storing things.

- Chapter 6 tackles the all-important pantry. You'll discover what pantry essentials you should have on hand and how to put them away so you can actually find them again when you need them.
- Chapter 7 will help you use your fridge and freezer in the most organized and efficient way, so you can store food safely and organize it for easy use.
- Chapter 8 is your ultimate guide to how to clean absolutely everything in your kitchen.

Finally, in Part 3, you'll learn strategies that will help you stay organized while you do what your kitchen is made for—cooking:

- Chapter 9 gives solutions for finding, organizing, and using recipes.
- Chapter 10 is the source for cooking basics, so that you can cook safely, quickly, and efficiently, while enjoying it.
- Chapter 11 gives you a collection of staple recipes you can rely on over and over.
- Chapter 12 teaches meal-planning techniques that will streamline the way you cook and relieve a lot of stress in your life.
- Chapter 13 includes tips and tricks on being a smart shopper—it will show you everything you need to know to be an organized grocery store shopper.
- Chapter 14 helps you serve your food in beautiful and attractive ways, and organize all of your serving pieces.

There's a lot to be done, so let's head into the kitchen!

PART 1   TAKING OWNERSHIP OF THE KITCHEN

An ORGANIZED Kitchen Is a HAPPY Kitchen

The kitchen may be the heart of the home, but it is also the place that naturally attracts the most clutter and mess. The combination of such a wide variety of items that need to be stored, the high traffic, the sheer number of pots and pans and dishes in use, and the high activity involved in meal prep can make this room especially challenging to keep organized and clutter-free. But don't give up! You'll learn how to organize your kitchen—and keep it organized— throughout the book. First, though, let's look at why your kitchen is so hard to keep organized.

Kitchen Chaos

Your kitchen is probably the gathering spot for family meals, projects, and meetings. If you're like many people, it also has more gadgets than the local electronics store. How serious is your disorganization problem? Ask yourself these questions:

1. Is your counter always cluttered?
2. Is your fridge so full you often forget what's hiding in the back of it?
3. Do things tumble out of your cupboards when you open them?
4. Do your drawers jam because they are so full?
5. Do you buy a bottle of ketchup only to put it away and realize you already had one, but just couldn't see it?
6. Is your freezer full of unlabeled mystery items?
7. Do you supersize your grocery shopping at a discount warehouse club?

If you answered "yes" to most of these questions, chances are you've got kitchen creep, the pesky phenomenon that occurs when items start busting out of their designated spaces. The cabinet doors don't quite shut all the way; the freezer door needs an extra good push to cement the seal.

The kitchen is a very difficult place to keep clutter-free because it's filled with all the things you need for the smooth operation and functioning of your household. The more stuff you have, the more you need an adequate storage plan. The key is organizing your kitchen so it fits your lifestyle. What works for a single person will likely be inadequate for a couple and fail miserably for a family.

Reasons to Organize Your Kitchen

We all have the fantasy of a dream kitchen—one of those tricked-out numbers packed with techno-wizardry appliances and clean, clear surfaces like you see in top magazines. You know that kitchen. You love that kitchen! You want that kitchen! Need a couple more entries to add to your "Reasons to Organize the Kitchen" list? When you put things in order, you can save money. How many times have you come home from the supermarket only to discover you already bought three of those things (whatever they are) the last time they were on sale?

Better still, by getting rid of stuff, you cut down on housework. It's true—up to 40 percent, by one study. Getting organized in the kitchen can save your sanity, save you money, and help improve the multiple uses your kitchen is called upon for—*and* bring your kitchen closer to that kitchen of your dreams.

Principles of Organizing Your Kitchen

Keep in mind that kitchen organization is not a one-shot deal. It's a lifestyle. You need to sustain it. It isn't just a matter of getting organized, but staying (and thinking) that way. There are bound to be a few days of backsliding here and there, of course. Life gets busy. But there are two keys to avoiding a major relapse.

1. First, it's necessary to employ a program of ongoing maintenance so that kitchen cleanup occurs while mess is still in the minimal—not mountainous—stage.
2. Second, it's important to take an inventory of your organization and storage strategies from time to time to ensure they're still meeting your current needs and lifestyle. Today's solutions may be tomorrow's problems, warns professional organizer Ariane Benefit.

Once you've completed the hard work of organizing that this book outlines, don't fall back into bad habits. Maintain the effort by always putting dishes, utensils, and pantry items back in their proper places. Shortcuts will only undermine your efforts. An investment of five minutes of daily touchups is all it takes to keep your kitchen clutter-free. Make these touchups a habit and they will soon be second nature. When tidying up, ask yourself if you really like it, use it, or need it before putting a thing back in its place.

Ask Your Kitchen to Do a Little Less

The kitchen is the center of home life for many people, and this means that many kitchens are pulling double (or triple duty) as a home office, homework station, craft center, and more. Before you can get a grip on the mess that is your kitchen, you need to make some decisions about how your kitchen is going to be used. If everyone is floating in and out of this room, bringing everything they need (and then leaving it) for all of their activities, you aren't going to be able to contain the clutter.

First, make a list of all the activities that happen regularly in your kitchen, including the amount and types of supplies they require. Activities that take a lot of time, supplies, and room are much more disruptive than those that take less.

1. _____

2. _____

3. _____

4. _____

5. _____

Look over your list and make sure it's complete. Then, make decisions about kitchen duty based on the following suggestions.

Move Some Activities Elsewhere

Ask yourself, is there a space someplace else in the house where this activity can be done? If there is another space, why are we not using it for that? Figure out what you need to do to make the other area usable. Maybe you need to do a little organizing and decluttering in some other spaces of your home. Maybe some reorganization of furniture will make space in another area. Or perhaps you need to make a space like a basement or garage more usable for these activities.

Decide What Your Kitchen Is For

Ask yourself, what activities do I really want happening in my kitchen? Some people love to have kids doing homework or crafts at the kitchen table. Others can't stand it. Maybe you're putting up with some activities in your kitchen because you couldn't think of another location for them. Decide what makes you comfortable and set some rules.

Where Will the Materials Go?

If you plan to continue using the kitchen for an activity like paying bills, ask yourself, do I have storage space in the kitchen for the items routinely needed for this activity? If you want to use your kitchen counter as a spot to pay bills, but there is no place to keep your checkbook, calculator, laptop, and bills, maybe this isn't the right spot for this activity.

Should This Be Done in the Kitchen?

Ask, is this an activity that makes sense to do in the kitchen? Some projects, such as flower arranging or messy crafts, really need to be done in the kitchen where cleanup is easier and there is access to water. Projects with less danger to your carpets can probably be done elsewhere. And some things really are not well-suited to the kitchen at all, particularly tasks that involve paperwork that could get wet or dirty.

Attack Your Kitchen Slowly

One of the biggest temptations in almost every area of life is to try to take on too much, too fast. This is a huge problem when it comes to getting your kitchen under control. Instead of trying to tackle organizational problems in small, manageable steps, people are often tempted to try to take on the entire room (or even the entire house) at once.

When too much is taken on too fast, people quickly experience "crash-and-burn" syndrome. You can quickly become discouraged, paralyzed, and exhausted, collapsing on a kitchen chair and looking around with despair. But it doesn't have to be this way!

Break It Down

Kitchen organizing feels overwhelming because there are so many things that need to be done and it seems like it will take huge amounts of time to complete them all. The key to getting past this is to break down your kitchen project into smaller tasks. Use the following list of projects and tackle one a day, a few per week, or a handful per weekend to get through them.

- Clean and organize one shelf or drawer in the fridge.
- Clean and organize one shelf or drawer in the freezer.
- Clear off and clean countertops.
- Clean the outside of one appliance.
- Organize one cupboard or drawer.
- Organize one shelf in your pantry.
- Organize your bulletin board.
- Sort and organize materials in one basket or box in the kitchen.

Each of these tasks should not take more than ten minutes.

Manage Expectations

Approach all of your organizing tasks with realistic expectations. You are not going to have a showroom kitchen by tomorrow. You are not perfect and your organizing work will be good enough by the time you are done, but it cannot possibly look like the homes you see in magazines. Don't expect more than you, or your kitchen, can deliver. Don't forget, you're limited by the size of your kitchen. By keeping your expectations in check—and generating only small, manageable goals, such as to sort through your plastic food containers one day—you are more likely to keep going, even when you feel tired. After all, small, achievable goals don't weigh on you as heavily as larger ones can. You know that your goal is realistic when it feels doable. A sense of despair is a good sign that your goals are too lofty and that they need to be cut back down to size.

As organizer Marla Cilley of FlyLady.net says about becoming realistic: "Perfectionism will keep you from ever getting out of the CHAOS (Can't Have Anyone Over Syndrome). This process of baby steps is all about progress, not perfection."

Push Back on Resistance

Stephen Pressfield's book *The War of Art* defines "Resistance" as the universal derailing force that seeks to undo us the moment we attempt to move to a higher plane in art, academics, relationships, and life. If Resistance had a voice, it would say things like, "You can't, you can't, you can't. You're not smart enough, organized enough, savvy enough."

If you are attempting to bring order to your kitchen, you can expect to experience some Resistance. It can come from the inside or from the outside. You might doubt yourself, and others might question your motives, especially if they are losing the war against Resistance in their own lives. Remember—it is far easier for other people to point out the flaws in your plan than it is for them to wage their own battles. It is also much easier for you to sit around and tell yourself that reorganizing your cupboards is impossible than just to get started actually doing it. Push past the Resistance you are encountering and creating and just get started; you'll soon find you're on your way to a cleaner, happier kitchen.

Ban Perfectionism

Perfectionism can paralyze. Sometimes it just feels so hard to do something if you feel as if somehow what you do will never measure up. Remember, the goal is not to do it perfectly. You just need to do it good enough for your own standards (not anyone else's!). If you set the bar too high, you'll just give up and decide you can never have a kitchen that meets those expectations. But if all you ask of yourself is to do a little better today and a little better tomorrow, you will slowly make progress.

Sometimes your kitchen projects may not work out. Remember that any improvement will increase your kitchen's usable space and make it a happier place to work.

Quick Pickup

Instead of trying to clean or organize the entire kitchen, try a five-minute pickup. Set a timer for five minutes and then focus your attention on the kitchen, picking up things and putting them away as quickly as you possibly can. This technique is fun and fast and will help alleviate some of the drudgery of cleaning and organizing. In a five-minute window, you can probably get all the dishes into the dishwasher, the counter wiped, the stovetop wiped, coupons put away, utensils stored, and potholders stashed in a drawer.

It can become a race against the clock as you seek to restore order in a minimal amount of time. It can also help curb the perfectionism that so often haunts you in the kitchen, because you just can't afford to demand perfection from yourself when you're trying to beat the clock. The other great benefit of a quick cleanup is that it can show you how simple it can be to tidy up.

If you find yourself sidelined by things in your kitchen you've been meaning to get to, scoop them all up and put them in a box. Attack that box on a rainy Sunday, but don't let the items in it derail you from doing a quick sweep of your kitchen.

Stay Focused

Often, when you begin to tackle the mess in your kitchen you're stopped dead in your tracks by a pile of mail, a recipe you want to make, a broken mixer you've been meaning to get repaired, and other distractions. While these items can be fun to work on, you need to remember that, during the five-minute pickup, thought is your enemy. It will slow you down and prevent you from being objective about clutter. This is not the time to perform deep or time-consuming tasks. It is just a quick buzz around the room, straightening and wiping things down.

Treats!

Another way to increase the fun of this activity is to introduce some kind of reward. You might consider putting a pot of coffee on to brew. As the aromatic coffee sputters in the pot, you rush around trying to create order. You promise yourself that as soon as the coffee is ready, you can sit and relax with a steaming cup of coffee in your orderly kitchen.

You can also use before and after photos to give yourself a sense of accomplishment. They help you remember how much you really did in your organizing and will help you stay positive about the work.

Eventually, you might find that order has its own rewards, but when you're trying to develop positive habits, it can be helpful to attach rewards to the tasks you dread, so that instead of thinking "No pain, no gain," you will be more inclined to think of your tasks in a positive way.

GOOD VIBES
in the Kitchen

Your kitchen is the center of your home—it grounds your home. If your kitchen is out of balance, it's likely you are as well. This chapter focuses on ways to make your kitchen a balanced, peaceful, and very personal space. The more comfortable and relaxed you feel when in the kitchen, the easier it will be for you to cook, clean up, and do other activities in the space. One way to help your kitchen become balanced—and stay that way—is by applying the principles of feng shui.

What Is Feng Shui?

Feng shui, pronounced "fung shway," is the study of energy and how it affects people positively or negatively. Feng shui is an ancient Chinese practice that was developed by agrarian people who recognized their dependence on the natural forces of the world. Feng shui, by integrating the Taoist search for balance and the Buddhist quest for harmony, seeks to incorporate these principles into the home, and specifically here, your kitchen.

In English, *feng shui* means "the way of wind and water" or "the natural forces of the universe." The ancient Chinese lived by these forces. Europeans call these forces "geomancy," and Hawaiians and Native Americans practice their own methods of energy balancing. The fundamental concepts behind feng shui have been studied and explored throughout history by people around the world.

Energy Flow

One of the primary principles of feng shui is that you want the energy in your kitchen to connect with the natural life forces outdoors. You must allow the energy to flow freely through your kitchen, and not hamper it by having excess clutter or by leaving things broken, including damaged or cracked windows. According to this theory, energy flows best along curving spaces—ovals and circles are preferable to jutting corners and straight lines. An orderly kitchen is more conducive to positive energy flow than a chaotic one.

Many people are initially quite skeptical about feng shui. Although some of the principles might not resonate with you, many of the ideas will likely mesh with your own intuition. It is as if they explain something that has never before been clearly articulated.

While some of the ideas associated with feng shui may seem a little odd and unrealistic for your own space, others follow the lines of common sense. Many of the ideas associated with feng shui seemed to be fundamental and universal concepts that can make sense to people in any life circumstance and of any religious persuasion.

While feng shui used to be thought of as a wacky invention of the New Age movement, people are increasingly becoming aware of the spiritual dimensions of space and the value of living intentionally in one's own home. Certain arrangements of furniture and home orientation evoke emotions—clutter can cause a feeling of helplessness, broken things can make you feel depressed and dark, dingy spaces can oppress your spirit. The feng shui principle that curving lines are more conducive to a healthy and aesthetically pleasing space, for example, makes sense to anyone who has lived in a shoebox apartment.

Principles of Feng Shui

The basic principles of feng shui are useful for those who wish to incorporate some of these ideas into their lives and kitchen. Many of the ideas of feng shui may resonate with you. Let's look at what these principles are.

Clear the Clutter

Besides taking up physical space, clutter can block new opportunities and keep you locked in the past. By clearing out your kitchen, you create space for a future full of possibilities.

Allow Energy to Flow Freely

Energy should be able to flow through your kitchen to promote good health and harmony. Avoid interfering with this flow with clutter or awkwardly placed furniture or appliances. Use round plates, not square or rectangular ones in your kitchen. Round plates have the most flow and support harmony in the room and during your dining experience.

Bring in Living Energy

Fresh flowers, plants, and bowls of fruits and vegetables improve the energy of the kitchen. Dried flowers are dead and create dead energy. Unhealthy plants create an unhealthy energy.

Contain the Energy

Energy needs to be able to flow around the kitchen in order to nourish you. Avoid situations that allow energy to rush through the kitchen and quickly escape. Doors in and out of the room should not directly face each other. If this is the case in your kitchen, consider hanging wind chimes to moderate and redirect the flow of energy.

Make Sure Everything Works

Stay on top of maintenance issues. Fix items quickly and keep your surroundings as clean as possible. Feng shui teaches that every job left half-done somehow reflects an aspect of your life that is incomplete and needs attention.

Be Aware of Energy Issues

According to feng shui, distortions in the electromagnetic fields can impact your mental clarity over a period of time. Experts believe that sometimes energy needs to be "rebalanced" by a trained professional.

Be Aware of Images and Symbols

Your choice of art, for example, is considered a message from your subconscious. Look around the room to determine what kinds of messages you may have unwittingly projected into your space. Consider changing your art to reflect more consciously your desires for the future. Instead of a print of a fruit bowl, hang one of a large happy family gathered together, or a print of a faraway place you want to visit.

Make the Kitchen a Center of Calmness

The kitchen is often considered the hub of family life. Make this room a contained area where you can prepare meals in peace. According to the principles of feng shui, the atmosphere of your kitchen will permeate the food that you prepare and serve.

Love Your Kitchen—and It Will Love You

Think of your home as a living being. If you care for it and nourish it, it will in turn support and nurture you. If you integrate some of the principles of feng shui into your kitchen, you may find that you can rest better, live better, and entertain more freely in your space.

Practical Applications

The first steps in healing your out-of-balance kitchen are quite concrete: Get rid of the clutter, fix the broken things, and bring a little more light to your room through the use of mirrors. Clutter is trapped energy that has far-reaching effects—physical, mental, and spiritual. All forms of household clutter can keep you trapped in the past, congest your body, and make you feel lethargic and fatigued.

According to the principles of feng shui, when you clear out clutter, you release negative emotions, generate positive energy, and carve out space to do the things you most hope to do in your kitchen. The idea that clutter holds people back from realizing their potential seems to be a universal belief, held not just by practitioners of feng shui, but by professional organizers as well.

One of feng shui's primary concerns about clutter is that it is not forward looking. Clutter is often a way of clinging to the past and it can be crippling to a person who wants to take steps to move toward the future. According to this philosophy, by getting rid of clutter, you create space for new possibilities.

Follow some of these practical tips to feng shui your kitchen.

- Feng shui supports the traditional kitchen triangle of stove, sink, and refrigerator because it promotes harmony. However, the stove should not be placed opposite a door, next to the sink or fridge, or under a window because this disrupts the flow of energy and creates a clashing of elements. If you can't change the placement of the stove, place a vase with water between the stove and the other appliance.
- Keep knives put away in a drawer or knife block to keep their negative energy under wraps.

- If the kitchen is visible from the main door of the home, put up a screen or hang something in the doorway (a curtain or beads) to prevent the energy from flowing out of the room and out of the house.
- You should be able to see the entire room when working at the stove. If you can't, place a mirror over the stove.
- A microwave should not be placed above the stove because it disrupts the flow of energy in the room.

Hiring a Consultant

Although it is fairly simple to grasp the basic principles of feng shui, it can take years to understand truly its underlying principles. Some people who intuitively resonate with the principles of feng shui and want to learn more, hire professional feng shui consultants who can come into their kitchen and home and offer practical tips for increasing energy flow and releasing trapped negative emotions.

Unless you are building a new home from scratch or doing a major remodel, the basic structures of your kitchen can't be easily modified. That said, feng shui offers practical, doable ideas for using smaller objects to change your space. These "cures" involve the use of symbolic items, color, and repositioning of furniture. A consultant can help diagnose the quirks in your home and help identify solutions.

The best way to find a local feng shui expert is through a referral from someone you know and trust. You can visit the International Feng Shui Guild at *www.ifsguild.org.* This group hopes to promote the use, practice, and teachings of feng shui. The cost of hiring a professional feng shui consultant varies according to location and other factors, so be sure to determine fees and services covered before bringing the consultant into your home.

Heal Your Kitchen

After you've begun the work of decluttering your kitchen, take a mental inventory of broken things and begin to make a focused effort to fix these or get them out of the kitchen. It is also wise to clean dirty spaces. Be especially mindful of windows, because according to these principles, windows are the eyes of the chi (the life force energy) and they affect your mental clarity. This is one of those intuitive feng shui ideas. If you stand at the sink washing dishes and have to look through a dirty window, you'll feel less happy than if you had an unobstructed view. Dirty windows strain your eyes and you have to focus to see out. They also can feel like a reproach every time the sunlight exposes all that dirt.

On a more basic level, smudged or cracked windows can interfere with your experience of light and beauty—instead of seeing your lovely garden, you might just see those flecks of dirt. The dirt might make you feel burdened and worried with thoughts like, how am I going to tackle *that?* These small things can detract from your experience of being in the kitchen, and can have a significant negative impact on your mood.

Feng shui teaches that the systems of your kitchen correspond to your bodily systems. You might have been able to guess that plumbing corresponds to your body's digestive system, so those who believe in this model would say that it is wise to repair leaky faucets and clogged drains promptly if you wish to keep *your* digestive system in good working order. Likewise, the electrical system in your kitchen corresponds to your neurological system.

When You Can't Follow Feng Shui Principles

American and European houses aren't usually built with the principles of feng shui in mind, so occasionally you will have a problem applying a principle to your situation. For example, it is considered good feng shui to have your desk facing a door. But if you have a desk in your kitchen it is almost always built in facing a wall. It is also bad feng shui to have your kitchen close to the front door or back door of your home. What should you do? In these kinds of situations, follow your own intuition (or the architectural constraints of your kitchen), even when they run counter to feng shui. You can also modify the effects of the problem, such as by hanging a mirror on the wall above your desk.

A Hospitable Kitchen

Another way to attend to the spiritual dimensions of your kitchen is to seek to be intentionally hospitable, to open your kitchen to welcome, feed, and nurture both friends and strangers. One way to enjoy your guests more is to allow them to help in the kitchen. Especially if you'll be having a large group over, invite a few friends to help with the cooking and preparations. When people offer to help in the kitchen, take them up on it. Working together in the kitchen builds and enhances relationship bonds.

One philosophy of homemaking that is slowly catching on in American society is *wabi-sabi*. This ancient Japanese philosophy is related to creating spaces that are uncluttered, adorned with weathered or handmade items, and intentionally hospitable. The elaborate rituals related to the Japanese tea ceremony are expressive of the *wabi-sabi* mentality, which has at its heart consideration for others.

If your kitchen is orderly and the atmosphere peaceful, it will be a place where people want to linger. After guests leave and dishes are being stacked in the dishwasher, the blessing of their presence seems to linger in the home. Some people believe that hospitable kitchens don't just strengthen those who visit the home, but also nourish those who dwell there daily.

The theme of hospitality is present throughout the New Testament. In the book of Hebrews it says, "Be mindful to entertain strangers because in so doing some have entertained angels unaware." This passage probably refers back to the Old Testament story of the hospitality of Abraham, through which Abraham and Sarah were likely more blessed than their guests.

The theme of hospitality is also present in the ancient Eastern Orthodox wedding service. During the course of this service, a prayer is said over the couple "that they will be blessed with wheat, wine, and oil so that they can give to others in need." The notion of hospitality is based on the idea that gifts are intended to be shared. By generously sharing your kitchen with others, you not only help others, you can also help yourself and help your home to achieve its full potential. A kitchen that is organized is welcoming to others and feels comfortable to you when you bring people into it.

Bless This Kitchen

Another way to increase the goodness in your kitchen is to do a kitchen blessing. Many cultures around the world have concepts of house blessings. Within Christianity, house blessings occur most often in the Eastern Orthodox, Roman

Catholic, and Anglican churches. Some people do not feel that a room is completely organized until it has been spiritually organized as well. A blessing is a way to do this.

Spiritual Transformation

The basic idea of a kitchen blessing is that space can be transformed through prayer. In most cases, blessed water from the church will be sprinkled through the room (and sometimes the entire home) by a priest while members of the family and close friends follow the priest and sing. A blessing can create an opportunity to remember every gift that has been given to those who dwell in the space, and also to remember that the family is much larger than the small group of people who dwell there.

Families stretch back generations and incorporate both the living and the dead. This is why prayers are traditionally said for those on both sides of the grave. Families can also extend beyond the confines of biology to embrace friends and the wider community. A kitchen blessing can help anchor people in this larger reality.

In the Jewish faith, kitchens must be thoroughly cleaned each year prior to Passover to remove all traces of *chametz* (breads, grains, and leavened products). The ritual of cleaning is a special one with a sense of expectation. See Chabad.org for more information.

A Native American tradition is to use burning herbs to purify a space and remove negative energy. A smudge stick (a bundle of dried herbs, usually including sage) is lit and left smoldering and carried around the room. It is moved along the perimeters of the space and into dark corners and the space behind doors, purifying the room with the smoke.

Blessing Preparations

Before a blessing, families clean their kitchens to a shine and prepare a meal, snacks, or dessert for those who will come. The act of preparing the room can be a joyful time, full of anticipation, hope, and gratitude. During the blessing, prayers may also be said over each area of the kitchen, as a way of consecrating specific rooms to specific purposes. In more elaborate blessings, crosses will also be drawn with olive oil on the four main walls of the kitchen. Within the Eastern Orthodox Church, an elaborate house blessing service is often performed when a family moves into a home, and then smaller blessings will be performed each January—after the feast of Theophany, when water is blessed and Christ's baptism is remembered.

The smaller annual services are a way of continually attending to the spiritual atmosphere of the space, praying for those who dwell there, and infusing the physical space with a sense of spiritual purpose. This might be considered a form of "spiritual housekeeping." Blessings are also a way for communities to celebrate all the gifts that have been given and the way that all these gifts come together in the home.

Your Own Rituals

Your kitchen is your space to practice your own rituals and ceremonies, formal or informal. For many people, the act of making dinner and sitting down together is itself a cherished ritual. Perhaps your family has a Sunday-dinner ritual, where you prefer a more labor-intensive meal and use good dishes and linens. Some people make their own bread and find that the weekly process becomes like a ritual. The thing about rituals is that they create order. You always do a certain thing in a certain way and it creates comfort and good feelings. In creating kitchen rituals you will make your kitchen feel more orderly and more like a space that has significance to you and your family; it will be easier to make the effort to keep it neat.

3

The **HEART** of the Home

The kitchen is the heart of the home. It's where people do almost everything—cook, eat, talk, craft, gift wrap, sew, feed the cat, do homework, pay bills, play games, and just plain hang out. Everyone in the family pops in and out of the kitchen throughout the day. With so much going on, you want this to be a space that is organized and focused so it can accommodate everything that's happening (not least of all the cooking!). Getting your kitchen sorted, cleaned, and stocked are important ways to keep it streamlined for family life, but the best kitchens are not only pulled together, but welcoming and inviting. If you make your kitchen not only neat, but also warm and fun, it will be a space that everyone will enjoy.

Pack Away Stress

If you want your kitchen to be the place your family flocks to, make sure it is a room that invites them in and doesn't push them away. Resolve that this will be a stress-free room! With a little organization you can keep stress to a minimum. Take a look at your kitchen and think about what you're seeing that makes you feel stressed. Take your cues from your gut. If the shopping list on the side of fridge just makes you worry about when you're going to find time to get to a store, that list belongs in a drawer out of sight. Don't leave bills on the kitchen counter—stash them out of sight. Don't keep your to-do list posted on the bulletin board where it constantly reminds you and others of tasks yet unfinished. Does your son's baseball schedule make you feel overwhelmed? Take it off the fridge and keep it in your desk drawer instead (or better yet, just transfer all the dates to your smartphone). Try to keep your counters and kitchen table clear. A clean kitchen is also an inviting kitchen. See Chapter 8 for cleaning tips.

Create a Comfort Zone

Your family comes to the kitchen because they identify it with comfort. Enhance the comfort of your kitchen to reinforce that. Use these tips to organize your kitchen in ways that help everyone feel at home.

Window Treatments

Fabric in the kitchen sends out vibes of softness. Take down the blinds and put ruffled curtains on your windows. Use warm and inviting colors. An organized kitchen has windows that are decorated in a way that complements the rest of the room.

Soften the Seating

Fabric cushions on the chairs, stools, and benches in your kitchen make it look and feel more comfortable and more together. Use a dark color fabric for cushions—it hides food stains and makes your cleanup easier. If you're considering a remodel, installing built-in seating makes a kitchen cozier and feels more organized (no chairs askew).

Shed Some Light

Another factor that can greatly influence the ambiance and functionality of your kitchen is how you have your lighting organized. Often homes have harsh overhead lights that glare on all who enter. Ideally, you'll have a few different types of lighting so that you can alternate them depending on your needs and the time of day. Invest in lighting that you love—lamps can work in a kitchen, as can beam or spot lights that will give you soft, steady light in exactly the place where you need it.

The way that you light your kitchen will have a dramatic effect on how you work and feel in that space. A change in the lighting situation can encourage you to get in there and start cooking. Soft, ample light can increase your efficiency, improve your mood, and transform your kitchen into a place of peace and hospitality.

Get Underfoot

Area rugs make a kitchen comfy and help to designate specific zones of the room. But to keep them organized and in place, be sure to use nonslip pads to avoid accidents. Washable rugs are easiest, but sturdier types, such as braided rugs, also hold up well in the kitchen. Avoid placing a rug under your kitchen table. It will always be covered in crumbs and you'll spend your life vacuuming it. It's also difficult to get one big enough so the chairs stay on it. Instead, place a rug in front of the sink, a large area rug in an open area, or a runner in a walkway.

Decorate the Walls

Blank walls are not exciting and what they end up doing is bringing the focus to any clutter you have on the counters or table. Organize any big empty wall space in your kitchen with framed posters, framed children's artwork, bright paint, a family bulletin board, or even a mural painted in a neat and balanced fashion. Livening up the space this way makes it visually appealing. No one wants to spend time in a plain white room, but they do want to come into a room that is colorful and interesting.

Tie into the Holidays

When you decorate your home for seasons and holidays, don't forget to dress up your kitchen, too. A basket of Easter eggs, holiday potholders, a bunch of daffodils, seasonal placemats, or a small tabletop Christmas tree are easy ways to make the kitchen part of the celebration.

Want to really dress up the kitchen for Christmas? You could have a small tree that has only food or cooking ornaments on it. Choose a gingerbread man or candy cane theme to decorate the room. Candy is a beautiful decorative item for the holidays—fill glass jars with colorful red and green candies and place them around the kitchen. Bowls of colorful ornaments are another interesting touch and offer an easy way to use decorations that you are unable to use elsewhere. The key to attractive decorations is to keep them organized—all snowmen together in one area, all Easter eggs gathered in a big basket, and so on.

Don't go overboard so that every surface is covered, making the kitchen hard to use and disorganized. Instead aim for enough to create a feeling of festivity. Store and organize your kitchen decorations in a specially designated box labeled "kitchen Christmas decorations," "kitchen spring decorations," etc. If you have space on the top shelf of your pantry, store your decorations there. If not, keep them with all of your other seasonal decorations.

Create a Reason to Come In

To make the kitchen the organized center of your home, you need to have things that draw your family in. They need a reason to come into the kitchen, and a reason to stay. Organize the following reasons to create a draw:

- Always have a bowl of healthy snacks sitting on the counter or table. A bowl of nuts in the shell that must be cracked to be enjoyed offers an activity and a tasty snack. People will sit at the table and eat, instead of going elsewhere in the home and leaving crumbs there!

- Turn on music or the TV when you're working in the kitchen. Your family will come in to see what you're laughing at or humming. Television can stifle conversation if everyone just stares blankly, so use any program as a jumping-off point for conversation.
- A stack of recent magazines, coloring books, holiday cards, or photos (neatly stashed on a shelf or in a cute basket) provide a draw into the room and give people something to do while there.
- Plants and flowers make a kitchen feel alive and inviting. For double duty, try pots of herbs in your kitchen as decoration and as cooking aids.
- Offer samples! Whenever you're cooking something and want a second opinion, or just an excuse for some company, ask for some tasters.

Kids in the Kitchen

If you have children, or grandchildren, they are probably naturally drawn to the kitchen. There are so many cupboards to open and things to explore! Older kids love kitchens because they get to assist with cooking or quietly work on homework with a beloved adult nearby. Keeping your kitchen organized when little hands are around can be a challenge but one that is well worth the effort.

Childproofing Your Kitchen

If you have little ones underfoot, their safety is your number-one priority in the kitchen. With a little effort, you can make it a room that is nurturing without any hidden dangers. An important part of staying organized in your kitchen is staying on top of safety precautions. If you follow the following suggestions you will always know the room is safe and organized for children.

- Install cupboard door and drawer locks. You can purchase these at discount or baby stores or order through websites such as *www.onestepahead.com.*

- Designate one cupboard for child-friendly items and toys and keep that one unlocked.
- Secure bookcases and shelves to the walls, so children can't pull them over.
- Keep breakable items out of your child's reach on high shelves.
- Use a locking gate on the entryway to the kitchen so you can shut children out of the room when necessary.
- Store cleaning supplies and things like cooking wine out of reach of little hands.
- When you cook, turn the handles of pots and pans away from the edge of the stove. Use the back burners as much as possible. You can also install a plastic guard that prevents children from being able to reach the stovetop or its knobs.
- Keep appliance cords out of reach at all times and consider unplugging countertop appliances when you aren't using them.
- Designate a set of play pots and pans for kids to use. If you let them play with yours, they will think they are toys even when they are on the stove or coming hot out of the oven.
- Keep oven doors, dishwashers, trash compactors, clothes dryers, and other large appliances closed at all times when there is a small person underfoot.
- When your child is in a high chair or booster seat, use the straps! They are there to protect your child from falls.
- Keep your trash can out of sight under the sink (behind a locked cupboard door) or inside your pantry, or use one that has a locking lid and is childproof.
- Keep remote controls, telephones, and other technology out of reach.
- Always test water from a faucet to be sure it is not hot before washing a child's hands under it.
- Move hot foods and beverages out of your child's reach.
- High chairs that clip onto the table will save you space if you're in a small kitchen. Be sure to follow all instructions and use the belts.

Child's Play

The kitchen can and should be a fun place for all children, but kids can bring a lot of clutter, so you'll want to keep their items organized. Use your kitchen table as a great place to do crafts, puzzles, or play games. Set aside some toys and puzzles that are kept in the kitchen. Some activities that kids can work on alone for a few minutes at a time are a great resource, so you can turn your attention to cooking while they are occupied. Stock your kids' cupboard with:

- Stringing beads
- Blocks
- Toy dishes and play food
- Dolls, animal figurines, and action figures
- Crayons, washable or no-mess markers, and some paper
- Toy musical instruments
- Shape sorters
- Books
- Reusable stickers

Keep these items organized in bins, baskets, or boxes that fit inside the cupboard or are attractive enough to set out.

Homemade play dough is a great kitchen project, and when that dough is not only colorful, but edible, you know there is going to be some fun! Making your own is cheaper and more fun than buying cans of store-bought dough (which you then have to find a place to store). Mix 3 teaspoons of cream of tartar, 1 cup of flour, ½ cup salt, and 1 package of Kool-Aid in a pot. Stir in 1 cup water and 1 tablespoon vegetable oil. Stir over medium heat until it becomes dough-like. Cool and use immediately.

Purchase a plastic box that will fit inside your cupboard and fill it half-full with uncooked rice. Add some scoops, plastic bowls, spoons, and small toys and your child will happily dig around in it long enough for you to get dinner made. This also keeps a great play area organized in one container that you can easily put away. Add new items to it occasionally to maintain interest.

The kitchen table is often the prime place for family games involving kids (and adults) of all ages. If you can stash your games on a shelf or in a cupboard in your kitchen, it will make for easy organization. If your space is limited, consider removing the games from their boxes. You can easily stack the game boards together in a very small space, or stand them up on a deep bookcase. Place the game pieces and cards for each game in a labeled zip-top bag, or very small plastic box or storage container. Decks of cards should always be rubber-banded, or placed in a zip-top bag for storage (there is nothing worse than playing a whole game and then realizing one card is missing).

Keep a small step stool in the kitchen; your child can stand on it to reach the counter, or can comfortably sit on it to read a book or play. To be certain it won't slide when in use, make sure the stool has rubber stoppers on the bottom. Keep the stool in a closet or cupboard when not in use so it is not underfoot.

Cooking with Kids

Cooking with children is not only a way to have fun, but a way you can teach math, discuss nutrition, and help kids eventually learn how to become self-sufficient. The kitchen is a wonderful place for teachable moments. And when you're cooking, there's a lot of talking, but none of it is face to face (i.e., confrontational), so it's a great way to feel close to your preteen or teenager. Tell stories about how your mom, dad, or grandma cooked. Talk about the kind of food you enjoy making. Ask your child questions about why he or she enjoys cooking. Use this as an opportunity to share with each other.

The youngest children love to squish things, so have them help make pie crust, cookies, and cupcakes. If some of it gets in their mouths, it's all safe.

Young kids also can have hours of fun in the kitchen sink, filling pots and bowls and "washing" them for you. Kids of this age love to be involved in food preparation. You can buy a miniature set of real pots and pans and cooking utensils for your child to cook with under your supervision, and organize them inside your Dutch oven for easy storage.

Elementary school–aged children are interested in reading recipes, learning to use the stove and oven, and being able to present dishes they've made all by themselves to the family. Encourage them to learn to make entrées, vegetable dishes, and healthy whole-grain baked goods. They need supervision with knives, hot items, and appliances such as food processors. This is also the perfect age for the Easy-Bake Oven. Set it up on the table or counter and watch as your child has fun baking without help.

Preteens and teens enjoy cooking and baking things that meet their specific tastes and interests, and if you have a kitchen that is well organized, it will encourage them to cook on their own. Don't be surprised if your teen experiments with vegetarianism, veganism, raw foods, organic foods, or gluten-free items. The kitchen is a great place to explore individual interests. Children this age may be open to learning family recipes and picking up techniques that will make their adventures in the kitchen easy and successful. Now if you can just get them to wash the dishes. . . .

Homework Central

The kitchen table is often the perfect place to do homework. There's a big open space, a parent nearby for help, and snacks within reach. This area is especially great if you have a child who needs a lot of help or encouragement to get that homework done. You can be in the room without obviously hovering. If you like having your kids do their work in the kitchen and want to encourage it, designate a drawer or shelf where you can organize paper, pens and pencils, a calculator (they might not be allowed to use it, but you'll want one if you're checking math homework), erasers, scissors, a pencil sharpener, glue, and a stapler. A small caddy (such as the kind used to organize picnic silverware) is perfect for storing these items and it can easily be grabbed and moved. It's really very helpful to have some Internet-connected device handy (laptop, iPad, smartphone) for those questions you don't know the answer to ("Dad, what's the capital of Montana?").

The hardest part about homework in the kitchen is getting your kids to pick it all up when they're finished. They have a tendency to float away leaving all of their debris on the table. Institute a rule that there is no TV, gaming, or Internet time until the kitchen table is cleared. All homework and books should be back in their bags, ready to go back to school. The school supplies kept at home should be put away in their proper place.

Your Other "Children" in the Kitchen

Face it. Your pets are pretty high up there in your affections. And in many houses, the kitchen also serves as a home base for pets. Their food and water bowls are in the kitchen, their beds are in the corner, and their toys are scattered around. They're no fools—they know where the food action is. And when you bring a puppy home, you're likely to shut him or her in the kitchen because accidents are easier to clean up there. Pets are definitely a big part of kitchen life and getting all of their paraphernalia organized will keep your kitchen clutter-free.

- Set up a designated feeding station so the water and food bowls are not underfoot. You can buy a special placemat to set them on. For large dogs, you might consider a raised food and water station that makes it easier for the pet to use and is also more compact for you (some allow you to store food inside them).
- Refill or change your pet's water at least once a day. Keep a towel or shammy handy to clean up drips.
- Do not store pet medications in the kitchen. You don't want to risk mixing them up with human meds or exposing them to humidity. Keep them in a utility closet or another area where there is low humidity.
- Be strict about pets and food! You don't want your cats jumping on the counter to help themselves, nor do you want your dog stealing chicken breasts from the table. Store pet food in the kitchen if possible. If you don't have space for large quantities, consider storing the bulk of it in the garage or basement in a storage bin and having a smaller plastic box in the kitchen you feed from and refill when needed. Consider keeping your pet's treats in a decorative canister or jar on the counter for easy access.
- If you keep leashes in the kitchen, a wall coatrack (piece of wood with decorative hooks) is great for storage. Organize the toys and chewies by placing a basket or bin they are to be kept in on the floor. If you're a highly skilled trainer, you may be able to teach your pet to pick them up and put them away!

- Clean your pets' bowls, toys, and bedding regularly. Use regular soap and laundry detergent. Do not use harsh cleaning chemicals on anything your pet has close contact with in the kitchen.
- The kitchen is not the best place for a litter box—who wants to smell that while eating? Find another room where it will work. If you must keep a litter box in the kitchen, empty it frequently and keep it as far away from the eating area as possible.

Office Space

A common use of the kitchen, particularly the kitchen table, is as a home office. Even if you have a separate home office, the kitchen table can be a very convenient place for paying bills, writing holiday cards, rolling coins, or setting up your laptop or iPad. The trick to using your kitchen as an office is keeping the things you need accessible, but not so that they take over the kitchen. A kitchen table that is constantly covered with magazines, bills, and paperwork is not conducive to family meals, or even family time. And if you try to eat at or cook on a table with papers or electronics all over it, you run the risk of spilling something and ruining them.

If the kitchen is where you like to work, find a place to stash all of your materials. A bench that has storage inside is one great option. A box that you can pack up and slide into a cupboard or stick in a closet allows you to move everything out quickly. To stay organized, buy some dividers for your box, so you can easily keep your papers in an order that allows you to access them quickly. Make sure you also have storage for pens and pencils, which tend to overtake drawers unless they are organized in a small box or placed in a mug in a cupboard.

If your kitchen has a built-in desk, you already have a designated space, but the trick is keeping that small space neat. Try these items to keep this area organized:

- Use a small vase or jar to hold pens and pencils.
- Place two small baskets on the desk, one for mail that comes in and one for mail that goes out. You can also use these baskets to organize papers and notes that come home from school with your kids and papers you need to send back to school.

- A small tray is handy for keys and sunglasses. You might also install hooks in the wall for these items.
- If your desk space has a drawer, use plastic organizers to keep stamps, envelopes, paper, charger cords, and computer ink neat.
- If you are keeping files in the kitchen, use hanging files in a drawer or in a plastic box.
- A bulletin board can be attractive and useful. Stick invitations, cute photos, dry cleaning receipts, gift certificates, and other important items on it.
- If your desk space is overrun with cords to charge your electronics, consider buying a charger organizer. This small unit plugs into the outlet and then has designated spaces for all of your devices to charge.

Other Kitchen Activities

The kitchen table is a convenient place to work on scrapbooking, sewing, calligraphy, jewelry making, and flower arranging. Not only can you sit at a table large enough to spread your project out, but as you work you can keep an eye on those cookies you're making for the bake sale. However, follow these tips to keep your kitchen organized as you use it for noncooking-related activities.

Sewing

If you're sewing in the kitchen, you likely have a portable sewing machine. And that means you are plugging your machine in from the table, leaving out a cord that can be tripped over; be sure you secure your machine and only keep the cord plugged in when in use. You'll want to make sure the table is really clean if you'll be laying fabric out on it, so always wipe it down before getting your sewing items out. Store your thread, needles, buttons, and other materials in a sewing storage box. The fabric-covered ones are cute, but the plastic storage cases tend to be more useful, bigger, and easier to organize. In a pinch, you can always stick it onto the seat of a chair and push it under the table out of view. If you have room in a cupboard or closet in the kitchen, arrange a permanent storage space. If not, find space in another room and make a habit of putting the box away every time you are done with it.

Flower Arranging

Flower arranging is also suited to the kitchen. If you're working with artificial flowers, be sure to clean up any loose pieces that fall on the table or floor. Fresh flowers are beautiful and likely require you to use the sink as you cut them and fill the vases. If you have a garbage disposal, don't send the stems and leaves down it as they can clog it up. Flower-arranging supplies are perfect for storing way up high in that hard-to-reach cupboard over the fridge. Unused vases can be placed around your home as decorative items. Consider grouping vases by color for easy organizing and also for an eye-catching display.

Crafting

If you're crafting at your kitchen table, be careful not to get glue or paint on your table or counters. Use a vinyl tablecloth to protect the surfaces. Store your supplies in a craft tote, basket, or plastic box and find a place where you can stash it out of sight.

If you're tight on space but want to keep some plastic storage boxes of games, craft items, or other things in your kitchen, a very tricky storage idea is to buy square or rectangular wicker baskets and upend them, with your plastic storage box hidden underneath. The upended box then becomes a decorative little table on which you can place a plant or a dish full of rocks you've collected.

Mr. or Ms. Fix-It

If you don't have a workbench, garage, or basement (or if they're full!), the kitchen can end up becoming a makeshift repair shop. You will want to keep a tarp on hand to cover the table or counter for your projects. A large wooden or plastic cutting board is also essential, and will protect any surface you are working on. Store your tools, glue, and other home repair items in a tool caddy, toolbox, or, if you have space, a kitchen drawer. A little brush and dustpan or a DustBuster will allow for quick cleanup. Don't attempt projects requiring power tools in your kitchen—you run the risk of sawing or screwing right through your work board into the table!

Without a Crease

The kitchen is a room where many people end up doing their ironing. If this is the most convenient spot for you, consider getting a wall- or door-mounted ironing board that folds away when not in use. Be careful when ironing. The cord from the iron can present a hazard and a tippy ironing board is a recipe for disaster, particularly when kids or pets are involved. Never put your iron away until it has cooled.

It's a Wrap

For holidays or birthdays, the kitchen table is a convenient place to do your gift wrapping. If you use this space for wrapping year round, consider buying a gift wrap organizer that will hang on the back of a door and store wrap, scissors, tape, and ribbon. You can also buy an upright, gift wrap storage bin that fits into a closet. Always make sure you're working on a clean table.

The Kitchen as Meeting Room

For many families, the kitchen table is where big decisions are made, plans are discussed, and confessions are made. It's the place you go to work through problems, calculate if you can afford a vacation or an addition, and really talk without interruption. In many ways, it is the place you meet to get other areas of your life organized, so you want it to be organized also. With a little effort, your kitchen table can be a useful place for a meeting of the minds. Start by clearing off the table before sitting down to talk. Turn off radios and TVs. The fewer distractions, the better. Create normalcy for the discussion. If there is usually a candle, basket, or flower arrangement in the center of the table between meals and projects, leave it there. If the curtains are usually drawn at that time of day, close them. Sit in your normal seats. Save the big discussions for after a meal is cooked, eaten, and cleaned up. Asking to have the ketchup passed in the middle of a talk about Dad's changing jobs can really loosen the focus.

Keep a pad of paper and a pen (or your tablet device) nearby for these kinds of meetings. You may need a calculator, too, if a heavy financial discussion is in the making, so keep one in a drawer (or have your phone handy to use that function). If you are having a difficult conversation with your spouse or teenager, a kitchen timer can be used to give everyone an equal opportunity to speak without interruption.

Create Kitchen Memories

Because the kitchen is integral to so many holidays and special moments and occasions, it's a place where memories are made. You can become organized so that you highlight these and build on them in many ways.

If you don't already have certain meals that are traditional for your family at certain holidays or events, start to create these. Keep a list in the front of a cookbook detailing family favorites so you will remember to make them again. When you make special foods over and over for the same holiday, they become linked to the special times you share. Not sure how to pick a food? Think not only about what is traditional for that holiday or season, but also consider what some of your family's favorite treats are. Occasions are the perfect time to serve these.

Enjoy the process, not just the result. Cooking together with family allows relaxed bonding time, and this becomes even more relaxed when you are able to spend time in a kitchen that is organized and streamlined. And when you work together towards a shared goal, you build memories. Relish the failures as well as the successes in the kitchen. The time you dropped the turkey on the floor will be just as fond a memory as the time you served it perfectly browned.

Work to preserve those memories! Take food photos. That dish you made looks too good to eat, so preserve it forever digitally and dig in. These photos are especially effective when you take a photo of the entire table, untouched right before everyone eats. You'll be able to compare what you made from year to year. Another great way to organize memories is to keep a kitchen journal.

Write down the dates and menus of special meals you create. You can make notes about who enjoyed which dish and write down how you might improve on the dishes next time. This journal also allows you to be sure you never serve the same thing to guests twice!

Create a Family-Message Center

If you live in a household with other people, chances are you all have very different schedules—and it can be hard to coordinate all these schedules. You might want to create a family-message center in the kitchen. This message center may include a large corkboard or dry-erase board for posting messages and bins for sorting each individual's mail. On the message board, you can maintain a food-shopping list to which all members of the family can contribute.

A family-message center can help ease stress that comes from miscommunication, because there will be a common place for messages to be left. Everyone in the family will know to check the message board so that even when schedules conflict, family members can communicate about upcoming events and household chores. You might also use the message board to leave kind words for those you live with. A little bit of kindness can go a long way to ease tensions and bring harmony.

Stores like Target, Staples, and the Container Store carry lots of great products you can use to create a family message center—from dry-erase boards and bulletin boards to baskets and filing trays. By buying individual pieces at one of these stores, you can customize your family message center to accommodate your family's unique needs.

Collages, Calendars, and Bulletin Boards

The kitchen is also a prime spot to create large collages and bulletin boards, like giant scrapbooks. A photo collage is a great way to surround yourself with the smiling faces of those you love and whom your kitchen feeds and to organize photos that are important to you. A bulletin board allows you to tack up (or use magnets on a magnetic board) ticket stubs, programs, invitations, cards, notes, and other meaningful items. Some families that love to travel have a large map in their kitchen and insert thumbtacks for every location they've visited. These types of memory-centered spots in your kitchen infuse it with your personality and help you remember the happy moments in your life as you work in the kitchen.

A big calendar with a different color for each person in the family is a fantastic way to be able to organize the family's schedule and stay on top of who has to be where. Chalkboard or dry-erase paint will allow you to create an erasable calendar on the wall each month. You can also use this paint to create an area to write to-do lists, shopping lists, or reminders.

Paint by Numbers

Color! It's one of the fastest ways to bring life and personality to a room. Painting the walls is obvious though. Think outside the box for some colorful and creative ways to infuse your personality into the room.

Create a design on your wooden chair backs. Scrolls, flowers, or even people's names are a fun way to liven up and organize your eating area (and chairs with names on them eliminate squabbling over who sits where). Old kitchen cupboards become new with a coat of paint and a fun design stenciled on them—you can even color code your cabinets so that the different colors signal what is stored inside (white for dishes, gray for pots, red for canned goods, and so on). The walls are a great space to let your creativity shine. Why not paint a family tree and hang little photos of each person by his name? A growth chart is a wonderful way to see how your children (or grandchildren) are really growing and changing. Get everyone in the family involved and paint a mural depicting a favorite scene, book, family activity, or location.

Let Your Personality Shine

A well-organized kitchen not only keeps everything in its place, but it also allows your distinct personality to shine through. Once you've tackled getting everything in its place, you will want to find ways to let your kitchen express who you are. Give yourself free rein to decorate this room so that it suits you and makes you feel happy when you are there. Consider a theme—birdhouses, antiques, sea glass, fruit, etc.—and use it as an organizing and decorating principle for the room. If all of your accessories tie back to the theme, or relate to it in some way, the room will feel cohesive and put together. Don't overdo it with your theme, though, since this can make the room feel cluttered and overdone.

Say It

A few plaques or inscriptions on the wall can personalize your kitchen and organize your kitchen philosophies so all who enter can enjoy them. Organize them into groupings or spread them out evenly along the tops of your walls near the ceiling. Consider some of these:

- Eat well ~ Laugh often ~ Love much.
- Cooking is love made visible.
- Never trust a skinny cook.
- Eat dessert first.
- For this good food and joy renewed, we praise your name, O Lord.
- I like to cook with wine. Sometimes I even put it in the food.
- Countless numbers of people have eaten in this kitchen and gone on to lead normal lives.
- Today's Menu Choices: Take it or Leave it.
- Meals and memories are made here.
- Real men wear aprons.

PART 2 GETTING ORGANIZED

4

The **RIGHT** Tools
for the **RIGHT** Tasks

It's a fact that people are making more demands of their kitchen nowadays, but we can't all have mega-square-foot kitchens with home-magazine centerfold allure. And we really don't need countertops the size of hockey rinks—at least not if we can slim our possessions down to size. It is the rare kitchen that is appropriately stocked with kitchen tools and equipment. Most people have either too many items or not enough of the right kind. The trick is in understanding what you need for what you will reasonably be doing in the kitchen. If you're someone who is cooking simple dinners a few times a week, you probably do not need a springform pan and an offset spatula. If you're someone who loves to bake, though, those two items should be on your must-have list.

Take Inventory

Start at square one by taking an inventory of everything you've got in your kitchen. You might have some kitchen tools stuffed in a drawer that your mom gave you and that you promptly forgot about. So you really must thoroughly go through everything (don't skip the cabinet over the refrigerator) before you can know what you need to throw out, donate, keep, or add to your collection.

As you go through your collection, you'll want to do some purging. Set aside anything that is rusted, cracked, stained, chipped, broken, or bent so it is unusable, or in any other way subpar.

Tool Time

Although they're usually small, kitchen utensils can take up a lot of space *and* they can really make a huge, tangled mess if you've got them jammed in a drawer. They also seem to multiply somehow, with strange tools you are unable to identify making an appearance now and then. They're so easy to buy, too—Julia Child said, "In department stores so much kitchen equipment is bought indiscriminately by people who just come in for men's underwear"—and she's right! How many times have you grabbed a fun-looking utensil while you were in the store to buy something else?

Utensils also tend to be odd shapes, which makes them hard to gather together without crazy edges sticking up. Taming those tools will go a long way towards making your kitchen neat and orderly.

The Necessaries

Some basic tools you may want to consider having in your kitchen are listed below:

- Instant-read thermometer
- Rubber or silicone bowl scrapers
- Whisk
- Wooden spoons

- Ladle
- Spatula
- Offset spatula
- Stainless-steel box grater
- Stainless-steel tongs
- Vegetable peeler
- Slotted spoon
- Cooking spoon
- Long-handled fork
- Kitchen shears
- Kitchen timer
- Vegetable slicer (mandoline)
- Garlic press
- Citrus reamer
- Basting brush (silicone)
- Microplane zester
- Wire skimmer
- Potato masher
- Pizza cutter
- Measuring spoons
- Dry measuring cups
- Rolling pin
- Kitchen scale
- Pastry brush
- Dough scraper
- Cookie cutters
- Baster
- Ice cream scoop

That's quite a list and you probably don't have, nor should you have, everything on the list. Instead, you want only items you will actually use. If you don't make bread, you don't need a dough scraper. If you don't eat ice cream, you don't want an ice cream scoop taking up space. Few people actually mash potatoes by hand these days, so that may not be a useful item for you. Look through the list and choose to keep items you actually use in the regular course of cooking.

Test Your Needs

Not sure what you actually use? Put all of your utensils in a special box. As you use them, wash and put them away in the drawer or basket where they belong. After two weeks, any tools remaining in the test box can be given away, or at the very least, stored in a hard-to-reach kitchen area or someplace other than the kitchen (for example, if your turkey baster is a once-a-year item that is essential, keep it with the Thanksgiving decorations).

Paring Down Your Tools

You probably have kitchen tools that are duplicates or don't work well. Go through all of your tools and examine each one. Is it in good working order? If there are any concerns about it (it's cracked, doesn't work as well as it should, has scratches in the Teflon coating), you should get rid of it. Count how many you have of each item. You should not need more than two of most items and for many things only one will suffice, particularly if you get in the habit of washing it as you work. All of those extra wooden spoons and spatulas are crowding your kitchen, so remove them.

Getting a Grip

All of these tools together can create quite the pileup. There are several ways to organize them so they don't take over the kitchen. Rectangular drawer organizers (plastic, metal mesh, or wooden) or expandable cutlery organizers can be used to create sections in your utensil drawer. All of your baking tools can go in one box or section, while all of your spatulas and wooden spoons can find a home in another. Do not overfill the boxes or your items will spill over the top and possibly jam up the drawer. Another choice is to put a nonstick mat down inside your drawer and lay your tools out on it. They won't slide around and will stay in place for you.

Be sure to place items you use most often in the front of the drawer. If you have very deep drawers, consider placing your utensils in boxes

Place a decorative canister or basket on your countertop with the utensils you use the most, such as spatulas, rubber scrapers, tongs, and a whisk. They'll be easy to grab and easy to put away. Be sure to place cooking forks with the tines facing down.

and stacking them, so you can remove the cooking box to get to the box of baking tools, for example.

If you do not have a shallow drawer to store your tools, you can keep them in a larger plastic storage box or upright in a tin or jar inside a cupboard. Another storage option is to place hooks on the back of a cabinet door and hang some of your utensils there, if they have openings at the top of the handles. You could also install hooks in the wall above the stove and hang utensils there.

Two-time your tools whenever possible. A pair of kitchen shears works for cutting up a chicken as well as for cutting coupons. There is no need for additional scissors. A metal spatula also works as a cake server. A cookie cutter can serve as an egg-poaching ring.

You may want to spread your tools out in different drawers or containers in your kitchen. Spatulas and wooden spoons are handiest nearest the stove. Baking utensils should go near any open countertop you normally use to work with dough or batter. Think about where in the kitchen you use the tool and store it near that area.

To maximize space, use nesting measuring cups and spoons. You can purchase measuring spoons and cups that are magnetic and will stick to each other in a small, neat pile. Kitchen tools with rubber easy-grip handles are not only easy to hold when you use them, but also less likely to roll around in a drawer. Bundle metal or bamboo skewers together with a rubber band to keep them together.

Cutting Edge

Knives are an important part of any kitchen. Martha Stewart recommends that every kitchen have the following knives: 3½" paring knife, 8" heavy chef's knife, and 8" bread knife. You can do almost anything with these three knives, but many people have more knives rattling around. Evaluate the knives you have. Do you need all of them? Of the ones you do need, are they sharp? If not, sharpen them with a sharpener or take them to a hardware store to be professionally sharpened. Are the handles in good condition? Are the tips intact and not broken?

A knife block is an excellent storage solution. If you are purchasing new knives, you can buy this with them as a set. If you are organizing existing knives, buy a knife block with the correct number of openings for your collection. You can also buy a knife block that mounts to the side of your cabinet, to save counter space. A wall-mounted magnetic knife rack is another solution which keeps all your knives in view so you can easily grab what you need. If you don't want to see your knives, an in-drawer knife tray (like a knife block, but flat) will allow you to organize them safely, out of view.

Pots and Pans

Your pots and pans do the heavy lifting in your kitchen and it's important to have good quality items that are stored and cared for properly. The first step is to take a look at what you're using for cooking. Your pots and pans needn't all be the same color or style, but they do all need to be in good condition. A loose handle is a recipe for a kitchen disaster. Rusted pots or pots with chipped or peeling nonstick coatings are health hazards.

Here are some basics you may find it useful to have to make the most of cooking in your kitchen:

- 1½-quart saucepan with lid
- 4-quart saucepan with lid
- Cast-iron skillet
- Sauté pan
- Steamer insert
- Dutch oven with lid
- Nonstick frying pan
- Stockpot with lid
- Shallow roasting pan with rack

You'll want to store your cookware near your stove, for easy access. There are two primary ways to store your pots and pans. You can stack them in a cupboard or deep drawer, or you can hang them from a pot rack. If you are using a cupboard or drawer, consider a pot lid rack, which allows you to stand all the lids up in a row for easy location.

Look up! Don't see anything? Well, there's an opportunity. Overhead pot racks suspended from the ceiling are a creative use of air space. Make sure the rack is securely bolted in place and up to the task of handling a heavy

> To prevent pots and pans from getting scratched if you are stacking them in a cupboard, line them with coffee filters to protect them.

weight load. Before going this route, however, consider the condition of your cookware. You want your display to enhance your kitchen aesthetic, which means your collection needs to be in spit-shine shape. Pots with scorched bottoms, dull copper finishes, or chipped surfaces are better left in cabinets.

Hanging-pot racks run the gamut of styles, from ornate ironwork to thin, minimalist wooden strips, to match just about any décor. Some have built-in shelves for lids or additional display storage. Creative homeowners have been known to turn some of these racks into conversation pieces. One homeowner converted a cast-iron register grill into a pot rack with stunning results. Another installed an antique wooden ladder and hung pots off the rungs.

Pot racks work best when hung over a kitchen island, although a wall pot rack can be installed on any wall. Julia Child famously had a peg board on the wall in her kitchen, with an outline drawn for each item so she knew exactly where to hang it. You will want to leave at least 40 inches from the top of your counter to the bottom of the hanging-pot rack. The key to using a hanging-pot rack is balance. When hanging a pot or removing one, you want to make sure the rack is evenly balanced; otherwise all the pots could slide to one side and possibly fall.

Bake Time

If you're going to turn out delicious desserts, you've got to have the right equipment to make the magic happen. Baking pans you should have include two 9" round cake pans, a 9" square baking pan, a springform pan, baking sheets, nonstick baking mats, cooling racks, a 9" pie pan, a muffin tin, and a loaf pan. If you aren't a baker, you won't need all the items on this list. If you're a baking fiend, you will also want a tart pan, jumbo- and mini-muffin pans, and a variety of different-sized glass baking pans.

There are several types of bakeware to consider. Glass is useful for pie pans and square baking pans. Ceramic pie pans are pretty to serve in, as are ceramic baking pans. Metal works for all items, but you may want to consider nonstick. Silicone is the latest in bakeware and prevents sticking. All of them stack well, but silicone has the benefit of being bendable so you can fold it over to fit into a smaller area. Don't stock your cupboards with *all* of these though! You may want to have a mix of utilitarian items (nonstick or silicone) for the heavy baking work and a few prettier items for items you are serving in the bakeware.

If you are tight on space, you can let different pans do double duty. The rack from your roasting pan can double as a cooling rack. Or, you can consider space-saving alternatives, such as using stackable silicone muffin cups instead of an unwieldy muffin tin.

Also, consider that you may be able to substitute one pan for another. If you have two (or more) pans of a similar size, fill one with water and then pour the water into the other that you think might be comparable. If they hold the same amount of water, the pans are interchangeable. Get rid of one.

Toss any bakeware that is chipped, peeling, or rusted. Even a small chip in nonstick bakeware is a problem as it means the Teflon is no longer stable and safe for use. Store baking sheets upright between dividers in a cupboard to save space and allow easy access. Other bakeware items should be stacked according to size.

Other Kitchen Ware

Now that you've got the big items sorted and organized, there are some odds and ends you may want your kitchen to have. Keep your salt shaker and pepper mill near the stove. Bring them to the table as needed if you do not have salt and pepper designated just for the table. Store olive oil in a cruet (a glass bottle with a spout), also near the stove. The big bottle can be kept in the pantry or other storage area instead of taking up space in a cupboard near the stove.

- Several cutting boards are essential. Plastic is safer than wood, since bacteria can hide out in the nooks and crannies of the wood. If you love a wood cutting board and like to have one out on your counter, reserve it for things like breads and never put raw meat on it. Use plastic cutting boards for produce and meats. As with other kitchen items, too many of one item creates clutter. Choose two cutting boards and label one to be used with meat and one to be used with produce. Keep another small cutting board for things like cheeses, nuts, and bread. Cutting boards can be stored upright or in a very shallow drawer.
- A glass measuring cup or a plastic measuring cup that is angled to allow accurate liquid measurements is something every cook needs. Keep just one 2-cup measure and get rid of your smaller ones.
- A colander is needed to strain vegetables or pasta. Consider a collapsible strainer for easy storage.
- Mixing bowls come in many sizes, but a big one and a small one are the bare minimum. Stainless steel is all purpose, but you may want to have one glass mixing bowl for recipes that tell you to use a "non-reactive" bowl, to prevent a chemical reaction with the metal. Always choose bowls that nest inside each other to save space.
- Potholders come in any design you can imagine. Choices include fabric squares, fabric gloves, silicone squares or gloves, or heat-resistant oven gloves with finger holes in them. These tend to multiply, so keep only four to six of them in the kitchen at a time.
- Kitchen towels will get you through cleanup. Be sure to have at least one linen towel for drying glassware.
- A trivet will keep hot dishes from ruining your counters or table, and if you choose a pretty one, you can store it hanging on the wall.
- A rolling pin (metal, marble, or silicone) is a must for bakers.
- Add pie weights to the list if you are a pie baker (dried beans work almost as well as pie weights) and store them inside your pie pans to save space.

Appliance Wrangling

Americans love their electronics. That countertop rotisserie, ice cream maker, bread machine, and slow cooker all looked pretty useful in the store, but they may just be taking up valuable countertop space if you don't use them regularly. Consider finding a new home for these appliances—either tuck them away in a cabinet or give them to someone who will use them. If you have a basement, garage, or other storage area in your home, you may be able to stash some of these in those areas for that one time a year when you do want to use them. To save energy (and money!) remember to unplug your countertop appliances when you're not using them. Even if they're not on, they draw a small amount of electricity. This will also allow you to coil up the cords out of the way, which will make your countertop much more organized

Appliances to Consider

If you take a walk through the kitchen section of your local discount store, you'll be overwhelmed by how many gadgets you can fill your cart with. They're all useful for certain things, but as the beginning of the chapter emphasized, they aren't useful if you don't actually use them! Here are some of the more common kitchen appliances you may want to have in your kitchen:

- An electric can opener is very handy; however some people just prefer to use a little elbow grease and use a smaller-to-store manual can opener.
- The microwave is a staple in most homes.
- A toaster can come in handy, but you might consider having a toaster oven instead since it offers more flexibility (you can bake many things in it and it takes less time to heat up than a full-size oven), as long as you have the counter space for one.
- A food processor (or mini–food processer) is handy if you do a lot of chopping, grating, pie crust mixing, or puréeing.
- A blender is also terrific for puréeing, and if you've got a thing for frozen drinks, you'll definitely want one!
- A coffee pot is like life support for many people and if you agree, then you need one.

- Some kind of a mixer, either a handheld or a stand mixer, is generally considered essential in a kitchen.
- If you can use it effectively, a slow cooker can help make cooking easier.

There are many popular appliances to consider, but some of them do things that you can replicate with appliances or tools you already have:

- Air-lock system for plastic food-storage bags. (Ziploc bags do a fairly good job of sealing in food.)
- Handheld immersion blender. (A regular blender can do the same job.)
- Electric knife sharpener. (A handheld manual sharpener does the same task and doesn't use any electricity.)
- Bread machine. (You can make bread using your oven if you don't mind a little kneading.)
- Ice cream maker.
- Pasta maker.
- Rice steamer.
- Pressure cooker.
- Ice shaver.
- Waffle maker.
- Panini maker.
- Fondue pot.
- Coffee bean grinder.
- Food dehydrator.
- Juicer.
- Yogurt maker. (Yogurt can be made in a very low temperature oven and doesn't require a special appliance.)
- Popcorn maker. (Popcorn can be made in the microwave or using a saucepan with a lid on the stove.)
- Rotisserie.

To create more counter space, mount your phone on the wall and use a paper towel rack that attaches to the side of the fridge with magnets or to the inside of the kitchen sink door.

All of the items on this list are fun to play with, but don't buy them or keep them unless they really are something you cannot live without. A general rule of thumb to use is if it is something you use once a week, keep it on the counter. If you use it once a month, keep it in a cupboard. If you use it less often, store it in one of your harder-to-get-to storage spaces. Haven't touched it in a year? It might be time to get rid of it.

Rethink all your one-trick pony items, especially bulky, oversize ones like salad spinners and waffle irons. It's human nature to respond to the latest and greatest come-ons. It takes willpower to resist. If you have a hard time, turn off the infomercials, skip shopping channels, and avoid sale days at the mall.

Dished Up

You've got to have dishes, but how many are enough? If you've got too many, you're taking up valuable cupboard space—not enough and you're constantly washing dishes. Consider what you actually use before buying dishes (especially when buying entire place settings) and when sorting through your cupboards. Some people only use mugs, so filling up your cupboard with cups and saucers is a complete waste of space. Only buy or keep what you will need of the following: dinner plates, salad plates, dessert plates, soup bowls, and cereal bowls. One type of bowl may be all you need, and you may just need one or two types of plates. For example, dinner plates can be huge; maybe you can use salad plates to eat meals from instead (this is also a great way to lose weight). Of the dishes you use most often, you may want to have two for each member of the household. For items used less frequently, one per member is sufficient.

For serving pieces, again consider how a typical meal is served. If you dish onto plates at the stove, then you can get away with fewer serving pieces. For most households, one platter, two vegetable bowls, a salad bowl, and a large serving bowl will serve your needs. Keep gravy servers, sugar bowls, and creamers in your kitchen only if you use them daily. If not, store these items elsewhere for company use. By the same token, unless you host large parties, do you really need to keep all that china you got for your wedding? Maybe it would be better given away. Or, if you do use it now and then, store it in an out-of-the-way place. That will help clear the clutter in your kitchen.

> You can help keep your kitchen organized by getting in the habit of doing the dishes after each meal. That means you need fewer pots, pans, and dishes in your cupboards.

If you have pretty serving dishes, use them as display items on shelves, plate racks, or as wall hangings. They'll make your kitchen beautiful and will free up some space in your cupboards.

Bottoms Up

Is your glassware cupboard filled with mismatched pieces, plastic cups your kids got at restaurants, and a mug for every Mother's Day since you started having children? It's time to streamline. Get rid of any that are chipped, cracked, or stained. Par down your mug collection so you have six or fewer (if there are others that have sentimental meaning, use them as pen cups at work or elsewhere in the house). Use sippy cups and travel cups designed specifically for children for your toddler and preschoolers rather than freebies. Ditch the plastic cups for the older kids and instead buy attractive melamine or a few pieces of small, heavy barware that does not break without considerable effort. Glassware is inexpensive at discount stores, so it's time to finally have a matched set. You'll want large glasses (12–16 ounces, called highball glasses) and smaller glasses, called juice glasses (8 ounces). Two per person in your household is probably enough. A nice set of matching mugs can liven up your morning coffee and make you feel like you've really graduated to real dishes; if you display them on a rack, it will save you space in your cupboard. Store glassware upside down to keep the insides dust-free.

Fork in the Road

Now that you've got enough cooking utensils and pots and pans to make your food and dishes to serve it on, you need something to eat it with: eating utensils, also called flatware. Stainless-steel flatware is most functional for kitchen dining and comes in every pattern you can imagine. All flatware may look the same, but there are significant differences in quality. Flatware is described with a number like 18/10. The first number is the chromium content. The second is the nickel content. The higher the nickel, the shinier and more durable the flatware. Beware of low-nickel flatware, which can leave gray scratches on all your dishes!

Take stock of exactly how many pieces of flatware you have. In my house, spoons tend to disappear (or get chewed by the garbage disposal). If you don't have enough for your needs, it may be time to add some pieces or to start over. Any flatware that is rusted or bent needs to be discarded.

What do you really need to have in your silverware drawer? Forks, knives, and spoons are the bare minimum. Other items include serrated knives or steak knives, dessert forks, seafood forks, grapefruit spoons, and iced tea spoons. If you'll never use these, don't waste your money or your space on them. Two utensils per family member is a good rule of thumb. If your family members are heavy users of some things (such as spoons—families with young kids in particular seem to use a lot of these), buy more of those items. If you end up buying a set that has pieces you don't use (iced tea spoons, grapefruit spoons, etc.), don't let them clutter up your drawer. Get them out of your kitchen—store them elsewhere or give them away. You can buy replacement utensils in your pattern from your silverware company (such as Oneida or Gorham). Check their websites for details. Replacements.com is a company that sells hard-to-find or no longer produced patterns.

Most flatware sets come with serving pieces or offer them for purchase separately. The most useful are large spoons, a pronged pasta spoon, and a serving fork. If you really want them, you can buy a butter knife and/or a sugar spoon.

The best way to keep your flatware is in a flatware organizer. Buy one that maximizes the size of your drawer. If the organizer is smaller than your drawer, a nonslip mat beneath it can prevent it wiggling around. Have a kitchen with very few drawers? Store your silverware in a set of matching jars, crocks, or containers, placed inside a basket or holder on your countertop. It will be easy to reach and will free up drawer space.

5

Shelf and Storage
STRATEGIES

The kitchen may be the heart of the home, but it is also the place that naturally attracts the most clutter and chaos. The combination of such a wide variety of items that need to be stored and the high traffic that passes through can make this room especially challenging. This chapter will explore a variety of ways to organize your cupboards, countertop, and drawers transforming your kitchen into a place of beauty, order, and simplicity, where you and your family will want to gather, cook, and linger.

Traffic Patterns

Keep in mind that the heart of every kitchen is the culinary work triangle, or the triangular alignment of the refrigerator, cooktop, and sink for food preparation. Making sure the layout dovetails with your food prep and storage areas makes for a smooth-operating kitchen and a happy chef. It also saves you time in cleanup. And let's face it: Who wouldn't want to spend less time wrapping up the leftovers for another day? You're bound by the constraints of your kitchen's architecture, but you can make the most of what you have by making sure your walkway between areas is clear and that you have adequate counter space near the sink and stove for food prep.

Organize Your Counters

In every area of home organization, begin with the basics. Kitchen counters often attract clutter, and this can lead to a crowded, defeated look. Installing small under-the-cabinet appliances can free up counter space. There are more options than ever before. You can find under-the-cabinet microwaves, can openers, radios, and toasters. Drop-down television sets, for instance, that flip back up and disappear when not in use are growing in popularity. Miele makes a sophisticated built-in coffee-making system that whips up espressos, cappuccinos, and lattes in no time. Of course, you'll have to think about whether you really need all those gizmos in the first place.

Attach a magnetic caddy to the side of the fridge to hold those pens that are always loose on the countertops. Use twist ties or rubber bands to capture small appliance cords and keep them tucked out of sight behind the appliance.

Try to empty your dishwasher immediately after the cycle is complete. This way, you'll reduce sink clutter (no dirty dishes will get trapped in a "holding pattern") and, if your family members know that the dishwasher won't be full of clean dishes for hours on end, they'll be easier to train to fill it.

Under-the-cabinet lights can brighten up and make your countertop come alive, and make it feel deeper because it won't be so dark. You may like to keep a tissue box in the kitchen, but leaving it out detracts not only from your décor but from the streamlining of your counter top. Stash it in a cupboard instead.

Dish Do-Over

If you do your dishes by hand, beware of the dish rack. Not only can it be tempting to let dishes pile up there, but the moisture can create an ideal climate for mold and bacteria to grow (unwelcome creatures such as roaches love this kind of dank environment). You might want to buy a stainless steel rack or any rack that is easy to clean and attractive. If you begin with an attractive rack, you'll feel more inclined to keep it looking nice—you'll be better able to see it as well, when you keep those dishes moving! A well-designed rack holds more dishes and keeps them neatly organized while drying, which also makes putting them away much easier.

Don't leave dish towels lying on the counter. It clutters up the room and they do not dry well. Hang them on a rack inside the cabinet under the sink or take them straight to the laundry area of your home. Sponges, scrub brushes, and dish soap clutter up your sink area. Stash them under the sink when not in use. If you want to have your dish soap out, decant it into a pretty glass bottle with a spout at the end, like the kind used to dispense olive oil.

Use Baskets

Papers easily pile up on the kitchen counter. Take-out menus, receipts, coupons, bills, newspapers, school notices, and more can overpower your kitchen. If you aren't careful, the whole room could be wallpapered in these. Place a basket (wire or wood) in one place on your counter (or in a drawer, if you have room) and designate that as the holdall for the loose papers that find their way into the kitchen. This should not be the permanent home for these items, though, only a holding place until you have time to sort them and put them in their proper places. Go through items at least once a week. This will help you stay on top of your kitchen's organization.

Cabinet Craze

Ah yes, kitchen cabinets. Everything in the world ends up stuffed in them. And sometimes when you open the door, there's an avalanche. It doesn't have to be like this, though. You can get your cabinets neatly organized so that you can easily access everything in them.

Categories Make It Clean

Before you get started reorganizing your cabinets, make a list of all the things that have to go in them. You may have small appliances, cookware, dishware, and more. Divide the items into categories, and plan to group like items together. So, for example, if you do a lot of baking, then "bakeware" will be a category you use. Or, if you cook on the weekends and freeze everything for reheating throughout the week, you may have many plastic storage containers. That would be another category. If you entertain a lot, you may have a whole category of serving platters and bowls. Go through all of your cabinets and group all of the items into categories.

After your kitchen items are divided into categories, determine whether each group needs cabinet space, drawer space, or some other type of storage. Will all of these items be kept in the kitchen, or will some items, such as candlesticks or fine china, be kept elsewhere?

So many people keep things "just in case." The problem is all these hypothetical uses get in the way of the real way you use your kitchen. The only "just in cases" you should have in your kitchen are emergency supplies, like a fire extinguisher, flashlight, weather radio, candle, and matches.

Next, measure all of your available cabinet space and make sure that the items you plan to store there will fit. If not, you will need to rethink your plan.

Purging

Now that you know what you have, think about what you need. That's right, it's time to purge. Go through each cabinet and find out what's lurking in the dark corners. All sorts of crazy things end up hidden in the back, behind or under other objects.

Throw out anything broken, unusable, or damaged. When you uncover your fourth colander, ask yourself if you really need so many and donate the extras. You cannot empty your cabinets out and expect to reload the same amount of stuff and have more space. It just can't happen. So if your cabinets are bursting at the seams, you must reduce what you're keeping in them.

Contemplate Space

Before you put things right back where they were, take a moment to consider if the old space is still the best place. As an overarching philosophy, you're better off storing items closest to their points of usage. Easy access translates into good kitchen organization. Saucepans, for instance, make the most sense if they're kept by the stove. Dishes and glasses should be near the sink and dishwasher. And you'll save yourself a few extra steps if you stack microwaveable containers near the microwave oven.

> Make your own pot lid rack. Attach small towel racks (the kind often found inside the kitchen sink cupboard door) to the back of cabinet doors. You can slide pot lids in them and the handle or knobs will catch and hold them in place.

A modest investment in stepped-up, tiered-rack shelving will keep items organized in cabinets so you can see and reach them all (for example, you can get step racks to organize your spices). Reserve tall cabinet shelves for oversize items. Set aside lower shelves for heavier items. They are more secure.

If you have a tall cabinet that does not have shelves, you can install them or buy wire mesh stacking shelves on legs (similar to locker shelves for kids, but bigger). These will allow you to create shelves and better utilize that space.

Reloading

When you're ready to load your cabinets again remember to organize tallest items in the back and shorter items in the front. Items you use the most should be the most accessible. Remember to keep things together in their categories: dining, baking, cooking, etc. Make the most out of limited space by keeping like items together. Store dishes with dishes, pots with pots, and serving trays with serving trays. Stack saucepans by size. The difference between neatly nestled and clumsy clutter is the lids, so install a separate rack for them. Stacking things saves you space, but consider whether you really want to move the stack of dessert plates off the dinner plates every single night when you go to set the table. If this is going to be a constant annoyance, it's not worth the space it saves you.

A Stretch

Virtually every kitchen is equipped with those tippy-top cabinets that are completely out of easy reach—that is, unless you're the forward of the New York Knicks. Those shelves are the Siberia of the cabinetry world, the place where lesser items are exiled.

Well, not so fast. Here are a couple of options to make that space more user-friendly. If you've got a tall ledge in a walk-in pantry, a sliding library ladder can make those oh-so-high shelves a problem of the past. Not so steady on your feet? Try a telescoping rod with a graspable handle. But don't chance it with anything too fragile or too heavy. A box of cereal, yes. A Tiffany crystal wine glass? Uh-uh. Use a good old step stool instead. Buy a step stool that folds flat and can be slipped in between the fridge and the wall, or behind a kick plate under a cabinet.

These hard-to-reach cabinets are a good place to keep the things that you use once a month or less often in your kitchen, but just can't part with. They're also a good place to store things like light bulbs, candles, birthday candles, cookie cutters, cake decorations, and large plastic storage containers.

If you're short on cabinet space, have floor space in the kitchen, but don't want to or can't invest in additional cabinets, buy an inexpensive, unfinished chest of drawers. Paint or stain it to match your existing cabinets and install matching handles and knobs and you'll suddenly have more storage space that will look like it was meant to be there. You can do the same thing by adding some open shelves to empty wall space.

Wake Up Little Susie

Inquiring minds want to know: Who exactly was Susan? And why was she so lazy? Theories abound, but the important thing is that her laziness led to an invention that makes our lives easier. The turntable action of the lazy Susan offers up 360-degree access to stored items with size-specific models on the market to match just about any space requirement. Give it a spin, and items come to you. Hard-to-reach items? Problem solved. You can buy wedge-shaped plastic containers to fit on the lazy Susan if you need.

If you've got a corner cupboard with a built-in lazy Susan, the trick is maximizing the space without using things that can easily tip off the shelf and jam up the spinning action. You also may have a very small door-opening to get things in and out. Place the heavier items on the bottom shelf. This is a great place to keep a bin of flour or a big jug of vinegar. A smaller top shelf is great for baby food, a kitchen scale, or glass measuring cups. Be careful stacking things on a built-in lazy Susan, since they can be very hard to retrieve if they fall off.

> Store birthday cake decorations (candles, matches, sprinkles, cake top figures, icing tubes) in a small colored box. The bright color will remind of you happy celebrations, and you'll have all you need in one place.

Expand Your Dimensions

Full-extension pullout drawers in cabinets will make pots, pans, and serving dishes easier to get to and offer up the ability to stack items more efficiently—and higher. Pullouts make reaching for items easier on your back, too—no more crouching or crawling on your hands and knees to get to things. If you install these, you'll gain anywhere from three to six more inches of usable space per drawer. Make sure the drawers you install have sides on them to prevent items from toppling off the sides.

In the Corners

Swing-out shelves from a corner cabinet will help you exploit every spare inch. Be sure not to fill these shelves too full because you don't want things to fall off as you're moving them in and out. Even seemingly little add-ons—like a tilt-out sink tray for your sponges and steel wool pads—can make a marked improvement. If you have a built-in cooktop, you may be able to install a tilt-out tray under it as well and you can keep cake testers, meat thermometers, and other little utensils in it.

An easy (and less expensive) alternative to buying vertical shelf dividers is just to use curtain tension rods installed vertically. They easily divide the space and can be moved around as you please.

Upright Space

Steal a wedge of space in a base cabinet and use vertical dividers to organize baking sheets, muffin pans, trays, oversize serving platters, and cutting boards in size order. The setup keeps items tidy and prevents dishes from getting chipped. Speaking of cutting boards—you can look for one that has a drawer built right in to store knives, or you might choose to have a custom version built that's set right into a cabinet drawer.

Plastic Problem

A familiar slapstick scene played out in kitchens far and wide is opening a cabinet door and being showered with plastic storage tubs and lids. A couple of pointers will keep the situation under control.

Note: Consider gradually replacing your current collection of plastic with either BPA (bisphenol-A)-free plastic storage or glass storage bowls with plastic lids. These storage solutions will not leach chemicals into your food. The new glass storage bowls are freezer safe and very durable.

One Shape Fits All

Buy plastic containers in a single shape. Go for square or round, but don't have both. Mismatched shapes will take up extra cabinet space and prevent you from stacking to the max. Mount a separate rack for lids inside the cabinet door and your shelves will look department-store neat.

Keep Only What You Need

Are you still squirreling away the plastic tubs and containers from cottage cheese, margarine, and soft cream cheese? Do you really need to save every last one of them? You may think you're doing your part for the recycling effort, but they're pantry-hoggers that aren't even practical. How many times did you store, say, tea bags in an opaque margarine tub and then completely forget what was in there because you just couldn't see into it—and, of course, didn't bother to label it? These items are not intended to be reused for food storage and it may not be safe to do so. Recycle all of these.

Pair Up Your Containers

How many orphaned lids and containers do you have? Probably quite a few. Go through your collection and play the matching game. Set aside those without mates. If you can use a lidless container elsewhere (for example, to store small items in a drawer) then do so. Otherwise, recycle or throw out all the mismatched lids and containers.

Keep Only the Best

How many containers do you have that are stained, cracked, or otherwise damaged? Say goodbye to these as well.

Stack Them Up

To maximize storage space, you should stack like containers together and place the matching lids underneath, which keeps them in place so they don't slide all over the place. You'll save tons of space. Place smaller containers inside bigger containers when possible—nesting controls the plastic monster.

Separate the Largest Containers

If you have very large plastic food-storage boxes—for storing holiday cookies in, for example—they can be a challenge to fit in your kitchen. If you only use these during the holidays, consider packing them away with the holiday decorations. These can also be hidden on the top shelf of the pantry or in a high cupboard.

Water Bottle Storage

More and more people are shying away from buying bottled water and instead are stocking up on refillable BPA-free plastic and metal bottles to fill at home. These bottles save money and the environment, but they can create a big storage problem. Try to keep two or three filled bottles in your fridge that are ready to go (store them on a shelf on the door for grab-and-go ease).

Additional empty bottles need to find a home in a cabinet, but they tend to be hard to wrangle since they are tall and tip over easily. Buy a shallow plastic, wire, or wooden basket and place them in it on a shelf. Another option is to place them on a nonslip mat inside a cabinet. Be sure the bottles are completely dry before you place the lids on and store them, or mold could grow inside.

Glassy-Eyed

When storing glassware, think like a bartender and line it up by size in columns instead of in rows. In other words, wine glasses on the left, juice glasses in the middle, regular glasses on the right. That way you're not reaching around the juice glasses in the front row to get to the water glasses behind them in the second row.

Label every storage basket, box, and drawer section so everyone who works in the kitchen knows exactly what belongs in it. Put the labels on the inside.

You can find some additional space by storing your glassware creatively with a suspended stemware rack. What an elegant way this is to display wine, champagne, and stemmed cordial glasses that are too attractive to hide behind closed doors. A great way to expand your glassware storage is to place a flat tray on top of your drinking glasses (as long as they are all the same size) in the cupboard. This will give you another shelf on top of them for more glasses. Just be sure you take glasses only from the top shelf first or you'll have a toppling shelf.

Drawer Do-Over

For some people, the idea of tackling those kitchen drawers can be almost paralyzing. There is just so much to do and it can be hard to know where to start. Keep in mind that you don't have to do it all at once—in fact, you probably shouldn't even try, because you might crash and burn. Instead, take it one drawer at a time—maybe one a day or a few each week. You drawers will be organized before you know it! Then it's just a matter of creating an ongoing habit of keeping your drawers organized.

One Drawer at a Time

First, think about how many drawers you have and what categories of items you have. If you have three drawers, perhaps you want one to be flatware, one to be plastic wrap and bags, and one to be kitchen utensils. And be sure to keep items closest to where in the kitchen they will be used, so keep your flatware in the drawer near the dishware cupboard.

To begin with, take a single drawer and dump out the contents. The incredible variety of items might even make you laugh. That's good! Enjoy learning about yourself and your own quirky habits as you organize. All sorts of things end up in kitchen drawers, and lots of them don't belong there at all!

After you've emptied the contents of the drawer, arrange the items into four piles. These piles can be titled something like "Keep in this drawer" (the things that need to stay in that drawer, according to your plan), "Move to another drawer" (items that belong in the kitchen but are out of place), "Store in another place" (things that don't belong in the kitchen at all, like a tube of glue, a broken necklace,

Chances are you can ditch all those appliance manuals that clutter up your drawers. Virtually all manufacturers have toll-free customer service numbers and representatives on call to answer any questions or troubleshoot problems during business hours. In addition, you'll usually find around-the-clock help online at manufacturers' websites where you can view the manuals online.

Gather together all the batteries you find floating in your drawers and put them in a battery organizer in a specific drawer. You can also buy wall-mounted organizers that include spaces for every size battery, as well as a battery tester. Test each loose battery you find—some may be dead, so pitch them!

and coin wrappers), and "Goodbye" (all of those loose twist ties, plastic cutlery from take-out food, paper clips, old shopping lists, and pens with no ink in them). As you reduce the bulk in each drawer, you'll find that it will be much easier to keep the drawer clean.

Junk Drawer Armageddon

Everyone's got one: a junk drawer, that is. Its very name almost encourages the abuse of space. Call it a junk drawer, and that's what's going to go in it until it becomes a pit of bottomless excess. How many corncob holders and apple corers do you have jammed in there, sitting under warranties for appliances you no longer own? You could circle the world with the rubber bands, broken pencils, and dead batteries in it. Using this space as a catchall will catch nothing of value in the long run. The junk drawer is a symptom of your kitchen's clutter problem. If you store like items with like items, there is nothing that ends up in a junk drawer. The reason junk drawers are unruly is that they're a dumping ground for every miscellaneous item in your home. If you define your space and start thinking in terms of keeping categories of items together, you won't need a junk drawer. You shouldn't have a drawer that has no purpose. As discussed above, each drawer should hold a certain category of items and only those items will go in it, such as serving utensils, spices, or flatware. If you have a junk drawer, sort through it and put every item in one of the categories you created for your drawers. The junk drawer will become home to one of those categories. Stop calling it the junk drawer and you'll stop using it as such.

Drawer Organizers

Inserting an organization tray or custom-fit divider strips can help subcategorize drawers even further and keep items from jamming up. If there's extra room, resist the urge to fill the drawer to the brim. And remember to go back and evaluate the contents from time to time.

Clean and Ready

Vacuum each drawer out using the hose attachment of your vacuum, then wipe with a damp cloth. Some people like to line all their drawers and cupboards with adhesive liner paper. The problem with this is it is hard to apply smoothly, without wrinkles, and often picks up at the corners. If the insides of your drawers are clean and smooth, there is little reason to use them.

If the drawer is hard to pull out, spray a little WD-40 oil on the metal roller mechanism to help it roll more easily. If your drawers are all wood, rub the sliding parts with paraffin or beeswax to make them slide more smoothly.

Place the keeper items back in the drawer using drawer organizers to keep things separated and neat. It feels great to open a formerly cluttered drawer and find that you can immediately spot the items you need—the boost in efficiency and ease of use will be well worth your efforts. Just try organizing one drawer and see if it doesn't make you want to do more!

It's a Wrap

Boxes of plastic bags, plastic wrap, foil, parchment paper, and waxed paper take up a lot of space, and if you store them in a drawer, can take up an entire drawer. If you don't have enough drawers to spare, you may need to get a little creative to keep these items organized. Wire racks on the back of a pantry or closet door are a great place to store these. A deep wire rack will allow you to store everything upright. You can also purchase a plastic wrap and bag dispenser which attaches to the back of a door and which you fill with your bags and wraps; then just pull out what you need.

Grocery Sacks and Totes

Grocery-store plastic bags and grocery tote bags are another storage problem. When you come home from the store, try to keep plastic grocery bags out of landfills as long as possible. According to the *Green Guide*, a newsletter covering health and environmental issues, Americans throw away 100 billion plastic grocery sacks a year. Use them to line small trash baskets in your home. If you can't use them, bring them back to the supermarket. Many grocery chains have plastic bag recycling bins right by the checkout counter. You can also do as many Europeans do and bring your own reusable bags to the store. It's an Earth-friendly thing to do. Keep the plastic bags in a dispenser, either a fabric one you can hang in a closet or pantry, or a hard plastic one that will mount to the inside of a cabinet door or to the wall. Fabric totes are best kept in your car, so you always have them when you need them.

Making a (Back) Splash

A hanging-organizer system can do a good job of helping you keep supplies at hand—and do it handsomely at that. It's strong enough to support spices or those eye-catching bottles of oil and vinegar. Sleek, stainless-steel versions are available to flatter the most modern of kitchens. Or consider a rail system that allows you to add on such accessories as a cookbook rack and utensil basket. Use wall hooks or magnetic hooks for aprons and towels and potholders. They're old standbys, sure, but they never go out of style, because they work.

Maximizing Space

You can eke some more storage out of your existing kitchen without doing a major remodel. Check around your kitchen for opportunities to convert idle space into workable storage. What's below your lower cabinets, near the kick-toe area? Nothing? Good. Retrofitting that gap might be all you need to store those no-good-place-for-it items like recyclable newspapers and pet bowls.

Storage in Plain Sight

Storage solutions work best when they add order to the workspace and pretty up the site. In other words, aim for form *and* functionality. One way to blend possessions into the overall design theme of a kitchen is to make productive use of otherwise wasted space. The areas under your shelves and cabinets are prime real estate. Got decorative tea cups and coffee mugs? Screw in some hooks and show them off. Bins, tins, and canisters on top of the refrigerator make stylish stowaways for unwieldy itemettes like twist-ties and chip clips that usually clutter up junk drawers. Some soups and sauces come in jars too pretty to toss in the recycling container. Rinse off the labels and reuse them. Clear jars combine personality with peek-a-boo practicality.

Slide out Some Space

You may want to consider building (or retrofitting) a cabinet, pantry, or closet with slide-out shelves and built-in power strips expressly to hold small appliances. Then, when you need to whip something up in the blender or pop some bread in the toaster, just slide out the shelf and use the appliances right where they are. It's less cumbersome, more utilitarian, and very time efficient.

If you've got a nice sliver of space, rolling pantry shelves are available, and the nice part is that you don't need to renovate, reconfigure, or even call in the carpenter to build them. These "thin-man" pantry caddies fit into the narrowest of spaces—even that slice of space between the refrigerator and cabinets. They roll in and out easily on a set of casters and come with a set of six fixed shelves. The small space between the fridge and the wall is a great place to stash big cutting boards, a broom, or trays.

Up in the Air

Grab some space out of thin air by installing wire baskets from the ceiling. They can hold everything from fruits and vegetables to coupons. But here's a caveat: Don't overdo it. Too many ceiling danglers can quickly make a kitchen feel cluttered and closed in, distracting from its streamlined appeal. Another up-high storage area people rarely use is the space above doors and windows. Install a shelf up there and put collectibles or containers with rarely used kitchen items in them.

Table It

When your goal is efficiency, every item in the house needs to be looked at with a discerning eye. Do you really need this? Would you really miss that if it were gone? Cast that discriminating eye on your kitchen table. How often do you really use it? Is it just a place to gulp down a quick bowl of cereal in the morning? It might seem sacrilege to part ways with a kitchen stalwart, but a multipurpose island could be the smarter solution. Imagine replacing an ordinary tabletop with a unit featuring a countertop or butcher block, drawers, shelves, and even a few cabinets or a wine rack. Throw in some barstools, and you've got a clever place to eat, prep, and store.

> Toothpicks on the loose? Corral them in a metal breath mint box and label it.

Another idea for making space is to install a tabletop that is attached to a wall and can be dropped down flat against the wall when not in use.

Install Some Space

A system of modular bookcases can hold your cookbooks, display dishes, and collectibles. The best part is that you can tailor it according to your needs by adjusting shelves, adding new ones, or adding inserts for such things as wine bottles. No floor space for a bookcase? Hang one on an empty wall. If you're really cramped for wall space, wall cubes offer compact storage.

Open Storage

If you have open storage in your kitchen, such as shelves or cabinets with glass fronts, you want these areas to appear extremely uncluttered, but that doesn't mean you can't use the space. Keep your dried beans in an antique coffee can. Store your Post-it notes in a little wooden box. Keep books of matches inside decorative mugs or vases. To the untrained eye this will look like attractive items on display, but for the stealth kitchen organizer, it is just more storage space that can be maximized.

Get Creative

Joe, a self-described junk enthusiast and avid antiques collector, moved into an actual antique: a home whose foundation dates back to the 1850s, when it was originally a Pony Express stop. Needless to say, the house has a few quirks—namely, no drawers in the kitchen. One solution Joe came up with was to keep his flatware in attractive Fire-King glass containers. They add colorful accents to the kitchen and are faithful to the vintage aesthetic of the home. Another plus is that when Joe hosts a dinner party, he just grabs the flatware jar and brings it to the table for easy place setting.

Let yourself be unconventional. One owner of a space-deprived villa in Florida never uses her dishwasher, at least not for its intended purpose. Instead of letting all those juicy cubic feet go to waste, she uses it to store her clean kitchen utensils. Not a baker? The oven becomes a great storage place for dishes and pots and pans.

Trash and Recyclables

What goes in must come out. This is especially the case with the kitchen. You bring in a huge amount of food, packaging, and other containers many of which will need to be discarded eventually. Stench and disarray can come if you don't have a good system for managing garbage and recyclables.

Choosing a Garbage Can

Garbage cans with lids are ideal for keeping bad smells in and pests out. Stainless steel can also be attractive and can endure for many years. If you purchase a can that uses a foot lever, you'll reduce the risk of picking up bacteria while cooking because your hands will never touch the trash can. If you like to keep your garbage can under the sink, consider installing a slide-out for it, so you can just slide it out, dump your garbage, and let it roll right back in place.

After your garbage bag is full, seal and dispose of it as quickly as possible. Keep a stack of garbage bags at the bottom of your can so you can just grab one and reline.

One of the biggest mistakes people make is overfilling the garbage can. This makes it very difficult to get the trash bag out without things falling all over the floor. If you're placing garbage in the can and the trash is at the rim of the can, it's time to empty the garbage.

Consider composting for your food garbage. A ceramic jar with a tight-fitting lid neatly holds all the scraps until you're ready to take them outside and prevents odors from escaping. If you're tossing food scraps, place these scraps within a small plastic bag that can be sealed and toss that into the larger garbage bag. This will reduce bad odors. Broken glass should be placed in a paper bag that is folded down and placed inside a plastic bag (you can't recycle broken glass).

To maintain a clean-smelling room, you may want to spray your garbage can with disinfectant spray (that also removes odor) and clean the garbage can itself on a regular basis.

Managing Recyclables

Recycling is a great way to reduce waste and to conserve resources. Most American cities now have dynamic recycling programs. Minimal effort is required on your part to make recycling work in your home. It's easy to do once you have a system in place.

First of all, make sure that you rinse all cans and glass bottles well. They can stink and attract pests if they are left with residue on them. Don't forget to separate out soda cans and water bottles if your state has a refund policy. These containers should also be rinsed out to avoid a mess when you are returning them.

In most cities, you will be expected to foot-flatten food cartons and plastic bottles and jugs. You'll also be expected to separate green, brown, blue, and clear glass as well as newspapers and cereal boxes. You may be asked to separate plastics according to the number on the bottom of the container. Check with your town or garbage service to find out exactly what they need you to do and follow their instructions.

If you purchase a recycling sorter with at least two separate bins, this can simplify your task. Keep in mind, however, that, like trash, even well-rinsed bottles and cans will create a sticky, stinky residue in your bin. The bin will need to be washed frequently. Where will you keep the bin? If there isn't room in your kitchen, a laundry room, mud room, back hallway, back porch, or garage are possible places to stash it.

Ideally, you'll take your recycling out as quickly as possible. If you live in an area where you keep large, color-coded bins out back at all times, you can simply store your recycling in plastic grocery bags and then carry them out each morning or evening. This is especially the case with newspapers—they tend to create a lot of clutter and can be cumbersome if you try to take out too many at the same time. Just as you bring in a single newspaper each morning, try to take out (or place in a recycling container) a single newspaper each night. By tackling your recycling routinely, you can prevent the work and mess involved in managing a larger recycling system.

Many people store medications, vitamins, pain relievers, and supplements in the kitchen because they take them with meals. The problem is all those little bottles can create complete chaos. Place all of them in a plastic or wire basket that can be taken in and out of a cupboard easily. They can also be stored on their sides in a shallow drawer. Be sure to place a nonslip mat under them so they stay label up. Regularly remove medications you are no longer taking or those that are expired.

Organizing Your Grill Accessories

If you have an outdoor grill, you probably have paraphernalia that goes with it. This includes tongs, spatula, fork, skewers, barbecue brush, and accessories like grill baskets, grill lighters, and smoking trays. One way to get them out of the kitchen is to put them in an outdoor cabinet next to the grill. You can purchase a plastic potting cart that has doors and a drawer to store these items in. If you have a gas grill, consider buying an extra propane canister so you will never run out of gas. It will fit in the cabinet. If you have a charcoal grill, you will want to keep briquettes and lighter fluid on hand as well.

Hard-to-Store Items

When your kids bring their lunchboxes home for an extended holiday, do you never know quite where to keep them? We've all got those items that don't have a permanent home in the kitchen because they come and go so much. Finding the perfect spot can take some thinking, but once you identify a place for each item, you'll always be able to put it away. Those lunchboxes and lunch bags can be stashed at the bottom of a pantry or on top of your baking pans in a cabinet. They need to be stored low enough so the kiddos can reach them when it's time to load them up again. Thermoses are another tough item. Keep them with your water bottles.

Then there are wacky utensils like nutcrackers, church keys, strawberry hullers, corn cob holders, shrimp deveiners, bamboo skewers, and manual can openers that rarely get used, but you want to keep. These are best kept in a basket or box on a top shelf of a hard-to-reach cabinet. If you have plastic cutlery for packed lunches, picnics, or outdoor meals, keep it in a zip-top bag on a shelf in a cabinet, or in a wide-mouth jar.

> Straws have a way of exploding all over the kitchen. Buy one of those old-fashioned glass straw jars with a metal lid, or just stick them all in a glass.

Keeping Your Kitchen Clutter-Free

Americans spend billions of dollars a year renovating their kitchens, turning them into status symbol jewels of the home. And then, poof! The sleek and streamlined super-kitchen façade is lost under a poor storage system. Clutter influences not only the kitchen but the adjoining rooms as well. With open floor plans featured in so many homes these days, a cluttered kitchen can affect an entire suite of rooms or your whole house. Be careful! Clutter is contagious.

The best habit you can adopt when organizing your kitchen is to give yourself regularly scheduled reality checks. What do you use? What do you need? Is an item worth the counter space or cabinet space it demands? Keep in mind that the best clutter-buster is the ability to *just say no*. Putting everything away takes a little bit more thought than yanking it off the shelves. It's crucial to have a dedicated home for every item. The alternative is chaos.

6

PANTRY Prep

This chapter is about organizing your pantry. Don't panic if you don't have an actual separate pantry (lots of people don't). Any place you store room-temperature food in your kitchen is a pantry, whether it is one separate space or several cupboards. It's a tough area to keep neat, because the contents are constantly changing as you use them and buy new things. It's also challenging because of the different sizes of the items.

There are many great techniques you can use to keep your pantry in order. By arranging your food in an accessible and easy-to-spot way, you'll find that cooking is simpler. You'll also be far less likely to be confused about what you do and don't need come grocery day, and you'll save money as a result.

Pantry Principles

The pantry is one spot in the kitchen that can get out of control, with boxes and cans tipping over and the one thing you desperately need hiding in the far corners. Taking charge of your pantry means not only sorting and separating, but staying on top of things so chaos can't take over again.

Take a good hard look at your pantry area. Are you using all the space? Are you able to reach every spot conveniently? Do you have stable shelving? Wire racks are best for pantries, but wooden shelves work also. Be sure to wipe off your shelves before you begin placing items in your pantry.

Trick out every inch of space with wall racks, door racks (either screwed-in, or over-the-door units), hooks, under-the-shelf hanging storage, tiered-step storage, and storage containers designed for specific items, such as a soup can holder.

Very large spaces between shelves should be used either to store very tall items, or should have shelves installed in between to make the space more usable. Another additional storage idea is to place a freestanding plastic box with a sliding drawer on a shelf. You can just pull the drawer out to get what you need, and you can easily contain a whole category of items inside the box. The drawer can be moved anywhere you want it at any time.

Don't store foods in cupboards where there are visible pipes. They can create condensation or even worse, leaks, damaging your food.

Lazy Susans are not the best choice for pantries. You can probably store more if you stack items or use storage containers. Be sure to make good use sure of the floor. Place large, heavy items on the floor (like soda bottles, large bottles of oil, or big bins of flour). If you have a good amount of floor space, stacking metal mesh baskets can give you additional storage space. You should also look up and determine if there is any place to install a hanging basket system, or a very high shelf.

The inside of the pantry door is often wasted space. Install some narrow shelves there and you'll gain significant storage space. If your pantry is one you can walk into, go in and turn around and look above the doorway. You can probably fit a shelf up there, or at least some hooks.

Remember, though, that a good pantry is not one that is jam-packed with the most stuff. It is one that uses space wisely and allows you to see what you have and easily access it.

Storage Systems

The easiest way to organize your pantry is to store like items with like. So all pasta should be together and all baking supplies gathered in one place. Make subcategories and keep canned fruit together with the canned goods and oatmeal together with the cereal, for example. Jams and jellies go within the general category of canned and jarred foods. Keep flours with the baking supplies. This makes it very easy to find something because there will be a very limited area where the item can be. If you have duplicate items, place the item that expires first in front, so you will use it first. Consider putting labels on the front of your shelves so you know exactly where items should be put away and where to look for things you need.

Organize by Most-Used

Cluster pantry items in the order you use them. The most commonly used ingredients should go in the front and at eye level so there's no noodling around when you need to locate something quickly. Store the gourmet (and rarely used) items, like mulling spices and edible decorating confetti you only use for special entertaining or holiday baking, in the back or on top shelves.

Gather up small, loose items and keep them in boxes or baskets or on the door in narrow, plastic, catchall file holders, so you know where they are.

Try Meal Packages

Another storage concept you might want to try out is meal packages. You store everything you need to make a meal or specific dish together, so you simply grab what you need from one spot. So you could keep spaghetti noodles and spaghetti sauce together. Or elbow macaroni, tuna fish, and cream of mushroom soup in one spot (for tuna noodle casserole). This arrangement can be a lifesaver on a busy night when you don't have the time or energy to figure out what you have that you can put together into a meal. It's also very useful when you are leaving dinner instructions for someone else.

Tip Top

The highest shelves in a pantry are hard to use. This is the place for those rarely used items. Divide the items you're keeping up there into categories and place each category in a storage box. That way you can just bring down the whole box, which is much easier than trying to reach and feel around for the one item you need. You'll always know where that cookie press is or how to find the bamboo skewers.

Pantry Plus

Most people simply do not have room in their kitchens to store lots of extras. If you are a bulk or sale shopper (or would like to be!), you need to create an alternate pantry to store the large quantities you're bringing home to save money.

Paint the inside of your pantry white. The light color will make it brighter and make it easier to see what's inside.

The basement is the first place to look. Pick up an inexpensive plastic shelving unit and use it for all your duplicate items. A guest room closet is another great place to set up some shelving. The garage is not a great place because of the temperature variations. This backup pantry is also a great place to keep those cooking tools and appliances you use once a year.

Tally It

Keep a list on a clipboard inside your pantry of everything in the pantry. When you use something, cross it off this list. When you bring things home, add them to the list. This allows you always to know what you have, so you aren't digging around saying, "I think I have a jar of peanut butter in here somewhere!"

Another really fun idea is to paint the back of the pantry door with chalkboard paint (which now comes in many colors) or dry erase paint and write your list there in chalk or erasable marker. Erase items as you use them. Consult your list when making out your grocery shopping list each week.

A Well-Stocked Pantry

The idea of a pantry is to have supplies ready to use when you cook. If you had to run to the store every time you wanted to cook some pasta, open a can of soup, or bake some brownies, you wouldn't get much cooking done. Your pantry should be at the ready so that you have just about anything you could need for your regular cooking needs. Here are some suggestions for what to keep in your pantry so you are ready to rumble at a moment's notice.

Baker's Dozen

Basic baking supplies include:

- All-purpose flour
- Wheat flour
- Bread flour (if you are a bread baker)
- Cake flour (if you are a dessert baker)
- Granulated sugar
- Powdered sugar
- Brown sugar
- Cornstarch
- Baking powder
- Baking soda
- Cocoa
- Solid baking chocolate
- Salt
- Cookie decorations such as colored-sanding sugar and sprinkles (must-haves if you do holiday baking)

You'll want to consider what items on the list fit your needs. If you will never bake bread, there's no reason to stock bread flour, for example. Buy only what you will use on a regular basis and if you plan to make something out of the ordinary, simply buy it in preparation.

Take stock of the supplies you have. Most of these items are stable for a long time, but baking soda and baking powder do get old; so check the expiration dates. If you have flour or sugar in the original bag, check to make sure it hasn't gotten damp or been ripped open.

Store flours, sugars, and cornstarch in clear plastic or glass storage containers (and add a small, terra cotta, brown sugar–saver disk to the brown sugar, which keeps it from getting hard and will save you money and the frustration of trying to soften it when you need to use it). You can buy square plastic containers that allow you to just slip a bag of sugar or flour right into them, but dumping the contents in makes for easier measuring. You want see-through containers so you can easily tell what is in them. You'll also want to label them well.

Buy large containers (6 quart) for flour and granulated sugar and smaller containers for the other items that come in smaller amounts. Don't leave measuring cups in your flour or sugar as you don't know what amount you'll use and you may need the cups for something else.

These containers are great candidates for stacking, if you have room in your pantry. Be careful not to stack too high or you'll have a leaning flour tower of Pisa. Your grandma might have stored her flour, sugar, and salt in ceramic canisters on her kitchen counter, but this not only clutters up the kitchen, the ceramic lids are not airtight, allowing humidity and pests to get in.

Prevent pantry pests (small moths that eat grains) with the Pantry Pest Trap, a small cardboard triangle, which traps them and which you leave in your pantry. To keep the moths away, store all your baking supplies in airtight containers. You can also tape bay leaves, which repel them, to the bottoms of your shelves.

Container Craze

The pantry is where you head when you're looking for jarred or canned food items. The basics you may wish to have include:

- Tomato paste
- Tomato sauce
- Whole tomatoes
- Diced tomatoes
- Tuna fish
- Canned soups
- Spaghetti sauce
- Canned beans
- Canned vegetables if you prefer them to frozen or fresh
- Beef broth
- Chicken broth (although these broths are now commonly sold in cartons)
- Pickles
- Olives
- Salsa
- Pesto
- Canned fruit
- Applesauce
- Canned pet food

You may find that you have other items that you use often and should keep on hand. Use this list as a guide to start from, not as a rule to follow.

Organize these into sections, with canned fruit in one area, canned veggies in another, jarred sauces in another, and so on. Always place the oldest item in the front: If you bring a can of peaches home and already have one, place the newer one in the back so you will use the oldest item first. Most people have other staples that are basics for their family, so think about what your family likes to eat and what kinds of things you frequently cook, like baked beans, canned artichoke hearts, anchovies, pickled peppers, and so on. One way to do this is just to always replace something when you use it and to buy two of something if you go to the pantry, need it, and don't have one. That way you'll have one in your pantry for next time.

You'll also want to have a supply of condiments on hand. Stock these only when you are running low on the opened versions in your refrigerator:

- Ketchup
- Relish, mustard (yellow, Dijon, stone ground, etc.)
- Mayonnaise
- Soy sauce
- Honey
- Vinegar (apple cider, white or rice)
- Peanut butter
- Maple syrup
- Worcestershire sauce

If you have many cans of soup, consider buying a soda can dispenser rack to store them in so they're all in one place and easy to access.

Create a designated spot in your pantry for each of these items, so you always know where to look. Group things like vinegars together so all the types are in one place for easy access.

Oils can be a big section of your pantry. The basics are olive oil and vegetable oil, but there are so many types of each that you may end up with quite a collection. If you have flavored or unusual oils (like pumpkin seed or herb-infused) that you use rarely, store these on a high shelf at the back of a cupboard. Keep the oils you use most often towards the front. If you use oil regularly and have the space, buy large containers and then decant as needed in glass bottles with spouts that you leave by the stove for easy use. You might want to place one category of items (such as sauces, flavored oils, vinegars, etc.) on a baking sheet or tray in your pantry. This will keep them together and make it easy to pull the whole assortment out to look through.

If you store juices in your pantry (bottles, juice boxes, or juice bags) they are probably as a backup to the refrigerated ones you have. These backups can be stored in a high or out-of-reach place. If you keep juice boxes and bags at room temperature in your pantry for use, these can tumble all over the place once the box or plastic wrapping is opened. Stack juice boxes on their sides. Juice bags need to be contained in a small plastic box. The straws have a tendency to fall off, so if you want them secure for grab-and-go use, stick a piece of tape over each straw as you load it into the pantry.

Jarred, bottled, and canned goods do expire, so check the dates and toss those that are old. It's not just that foods lose their flavor after their expiration dates. They can turn your stomach—or worse. Also get rid of any canned goods that are dented. The dent can create microscopic holes which can lead to contamination of the food.

It's likely you have some things lingering in your pantry that you won't ever use. Maybe you bought two jars of a brand of spaghetti sauce and didn't care for the one jar you tried. Or you might have grabbed the wrong kind of beans and didn't realize it before you got it home. Donate these items. All they're doing is taking up space you desperately need.

The problem with jars and cans is they tend to get lost on shelves. Purchase a graduated step organizer and you'll be able to see everything. It's tempting to stack cans, but they might topple if you do. If you must stack them to save space, place a cutting board, baking tray, or even a piece of cardboard between the layers. It adds stability and makes it easy to remove the top layer if you need to get at something on the bottom.

Before reorganizing your cans and jars, wipe the bottoms and sides down. Honey in particular can get very sticky and end up making the entire shelf a giant mess.

> Make a date with yourself every six months to reassess the items in your pantry. This will allow you to get rid of expired goods and evaluate whether you need to buy some more staples.

Dried Dos

Who can survive without dried pasta or rice on hand? These are so important for desperation dinners that you'll want to be sure you have a nice stock of them in your pantry. Many people keep only white rice, but brown rice has many more nutrients and more fiber. If you're into rice, you might want to have other types on hand, such as jasmine, black, arborio, or wild.

Rice

Rice is usually sold in bags or boxes. Most bags are not resealable, which creates a problem. The boxes are also problematic because the box is usually bigger than the actual amount of rice inside. Transfer these items to plastic or glass jars and label them. If you need the cooking instructions from the box, rip or cut that section off and tape it to the container. Be sure to label the containers because it is easy to mix up the different types of rice if you don't look at them closely.

Pasta

Pasta can be another unwieldy item. There are so many types that you can end up with an entire cupboard full of just pasta. The most commonly stocked kinds include:

- Spaghetti (thin or regular)
- Elbow macaroni
- Penne
- Angel hair
- Fettucine
- Lasagna
- Tortellini
- Egg noodles
- Fusilli

There are probably 100 other types you can buy. To control your pasta problem, buy only one box of each type at a time (unless there's a buy one, get one sale). Use it and replace it. If you have tons of boxes now, work on whittling down your collection. Keep some standards on hand, but only buy special types when you have a specific need for them.

The best way to store pasta is in glass or plastic containers (Wal-Mart sells big glass jars and Bed Bath & Beyond carries many clear storage items). For the long noodles, like spaghetti or lasagna, a very tall, glass pasta jar is a good bet (Ikea sells tall see-through containers meant for this).

A big problem with pasta is what to do if you don't use the whole box, but the excess is not enough for another entire meal. If you find yourself with a handful of this and a handful of that, use it all together in a crazy mixed-up pasta dish. You'll want to pay attention to the cooking times for the different varieties because, for example, elbows cook faster than penne; you don't want to just dump them all in a pot.

Other Dried Foods

If you buy pasta mixes, dried potatoes, or other convenience foods, they are best stored in their boxes, stacked on their sides. Dried beans, nuts, and dried fruit often come in resealable jars, bags, or containers. Store the jars and containers on the shelves. Take the resealable bags and store them all in a plastic bin, so they are all together. If you buy sauce or gravy mixes in plastic packets, control them all inside a plastic zip-top bag.

Coffee and Other Beverages

Coffee beans and grounds last longer in the freezer, so don't keep them in your pantry. Tea bags and loose teas can be a pantry challenge. If you have a large assortment of teas, purchase a clear plastic tea-storage box that allows you to separate the individual tea packets (taken out of the boxes) into sections and clearly see what you have. Cocoa mixes that come in tubs store well in their original containers. If you're buying individual packets of cocoa or drink mixes like Kool-Aid, they can be organized in a plastic box or zip-top bag. You can also clip them together with a chip clip.

Snack Zone

Snack time! The specific types of crackers, cookies, snacks, and cereals you stock is a matter of personal taste, but no matter what you buy, you probably encounter common storage woes for these items.

Crackers

You can buy a plastic storage box meant for a sleeve of crackers, but the problem is that if you have half or fewer left, there's more air in the box than crackers and they will get stale. The better choice is to store an opened sleeve of crackers or cookies in a zip-top bag (from which you can remove all air), then place the food back in its original box.

Cereal

For cereal, store in a plastic or glass container. This not only keeps it fresh, but allows you to see exactly how much is left (no more grabbing a box only to find just crumbs inside). If you have individual packets of oatmeal and other instant cereals, store them standing up in a plastic or metal storage container or basket.

Other Snack Foods

Snack foods that come in bags are best left in bags and secured with a chip clip. Snacks such as granola bars and fruit bars can be stored in a plastic bin. You can also take those big bags of snacks and divide them up into individual portions in sandwich or snack-size zip-top bags. This makes it easier to grab and go and also helps you know exactly how much you have left (who knows what's lingering in that big snack bag; it could be a handful or a big bowlful). Keep nuts in the tubs or jars they come in for best results.

> An inexpensive alternative to overpriced chip clips is to just roll the bag down and secure with a rubber band. Or steal a plastic binder clip from your home office.

Rooting for Veggies

Onions, potatoes, garlic, and rutabagas like to be kept in cool dark places. It is not a good idea to store these in hanging baskets or countertop baskets because they are exposed to heat and light, which can cause them to spoil faster. A mesh basket or container in the pantry is a great place for them. If you don't have room, root veggies are very happy in the basement.

Take potatoes out of the plastic bags in which you purchased them. They will last longer if they can breathe. Once potatoes or onions begin to sprout, throw them out. Cut off any green sections on potatoes before eating. Throw out any potatoes or onions that are soft, wrinkled, or mushy.

Garlic can be stored in a garlic jar (a ceramic jar with holes in it); however, many of these don't have an opening wide enough to allow you to place a whole head of garlic in them. It will reduce its shelf life, but you might need to break the garlic down before storing it.

> Download the Pantry app from *www.thinkfresher.com* and it will track your pantry stock and transfer items to your shopping list when you use them.

Daily Bread

Long gone is the day of the bread box. One of the problems with storing baked goods is that if you keep them in the pantry, they get stale more quickly. If you store them in the refrigerator, they can dry out. If you freeze them, you must defrost them, and risk drying them out. The solution? Keep sandwich bread in the fridge; bagels, muffins, rolls, croissants, and dinner bread that you won't be using that day in the freezer; and items like brownies or cookies tightly covered or sealed in the pantry. If you have cookies you want to last a long time, they will freeze well in a large plastic storage container. Pies must be refrigerated and cakes fare best in the fridge as well.

Breadcrumbs that you purchase in canisters can be stored in their original canisters, but if you like to be able to see how much you have left, transfer to a clear plastic or glass container. If you make your own breadcrumbs, they are best kept in the freezer because they are more perishable than store-bought breadcrumbs.

If someone in your family is on a special diet (such as gluten- or lactose-free, or for nut allergies), consider setting up a separate section of your pantry for him or her, where foods that are safe can be kept together for easy access. This also prevents cross-contamination and reduces the temptation to eat something potentially harmful.

Spice Things Up

Spices are your friends. You can take just about any dish, work some magic with the spice rack and end up with a flavorful and delicious item. A well-stocked spice cabinet makes cooking a breeze. Some of the most important herbs and spices you may want to have on hand are:

- Allspice
- Basil
- Bay leaves

- Cayenne
- Chili powder
- Cinnamon—ground and stick
- Cloves
- Cumin
- Curry powder
- Dill
- Garlic powder
- Ginger—ground
- Nutmeg—ground
- Onion powder
- Oregano
- Paprika
- Black peppercorns (for your pepper grinder)
- Red pepper flakes
- Rosemary
- Saffron
- Sage
- Tarragon
- Thyme
- Vanilla—extract (*not* vanilla flavoring) and beans

Use this list to help you weed out items you have that are not generally useful. There are many great spice mixes and blends you can buy as well that are very convenient and useful. Taco or fajita spice mixes, herbes de Provence, apple pie spice, Italian or Greek seasoning, and Chinese five spice powder are some great examples of mixes that will reduce your storage space if you stock them instead of the individual spices that go into them.

Storing Spices

The idea of a display spice rack is outdated. Your spices will last longer if you keep them away from light, heat, and moisture, so displaying them out in your kitchen isn't wise. Wire racks on the inside of your pantry or on the inside of a cupboard door work well. You can also store your spice bottles in a plastic box, but make sure you label the tops of the bottles so you can find them. You can buy an organizer that will allow you to keep your spices on their sides in a drawer as well.

While it's nice to have all your spices in matching jars, it's not necessary. What you don't want is a mishmash of short and tall jars, so things can get hidden behind other items.

Consider storing spices alphabetically. It makes it much easier to find them and easy to put them back where they go. However, you might find you prefer to group them into categories like baking spices, ethnic spices, extracts, etc.

Keeping Track of Expiration Dates

Spices are not meant to be kept for decades. They lose their flavors and freshness. You should replace them about every three years. Make sure you are replacing, not just dumping fresh spices into the jars on top of the old spices! When you buy a new spice or refill a jar you have, put a piece of masking tape or a sticker on the bottom with the date, so you can tell how old the spice is.

Paper Products

Most people use paper napkins and paper towels in their daily life, but they're bulky and hard to store. Have one paper towel roll on your holder and have one for backup (if you buy in bulk, store the others in the basement or garage). Store the roll standing up or on its side on a shelf. A space-saving trick is to install a dowel coming out from the wall high up in your pantry (by the ceiling) and stick the extra roll over it.

Paper napkins are best controlled in a napkin holder or dispenser, but most won't hold the 500 napkins you get at a time in a package. Take the extras and stack them in a basket. Paper plates and cups are likely not items you are using every day, so consider moving them to the basement or other storage area.

Watch Your Wine

Wine refrigerators are perfect for sommelier wannabes, but if you imbibe only now and again and can't justify the investment, you need accessible storage. Keep wine in a dark place that is free of vibrations (read: not in your exercise room or woodworking shop). Make sure the room is at a relatively stable humidity level and at a consistent temperature. About 55°F is ideal. Basements work well. If you don't have a basement, your pantry is a good spot.

Keep all of your related wine supplies together in one area in your kitchen. Some of the supplies you'll want on hand include a bottle opener, bottle stoppers, corkscrew, and foil cutter. Some wine racks have special shelves or cabinets to store these accessories.

If you don't have a special wine storage area, you can store your wine bottles, on their sides, in your pantry. To prevent them from rolling around, take two pieces of wood and make an "X" (cutting out one piece to fit the other through it) on the shelf, facing out. Place one open side of it against the edge of the pantry or cabinet. If the other open side is not against the other wall, then attach a piece of wood to it to give it a side. This gives you storage space for about eight bottles (two in each "X") and they won't move.

7

FRIDGE and FREEZER Fun

Your fridge and freezer are essential to your kitchen. Learning how to package and store food safely will protect you and your family. Keeping the fridge and freezer organized will allow you to actually see (and use) what you have stored, thereby saving you money. Don't be like anthropologist Edward T. Hall who said, "I may be able to spot arrowheads on the desert, but a refrigerator is a jungle in which I am easily lost." Keeping the fridge orderly will also keep you sane. You truly can lose your mind if you can't find the yogurt you *know* you bought. An organized fridge also keeps away what my family calls the cranky old man. When my side-by-side fridge gets overstuffed, disorganized and messy, things have a tendency to just fall out when you open the door. We say there's a cranky old man living in there, throwing things at us. Keep the old man away by keeping your fridge neat!

Chillin'

The first step in organizing your refrigerator and freezer is to empty them out and clean them. Start on the top shelf. Decide what will be kept; then throw away old leftovers and let go of items that you know you'll never eat. Open all containers and check what's inside. Throw out anything that's questionable or past its expiration date. Be ruthless. The lingonberry jelly you bought for a recipe two years ago might not be expired, but are you ever really going to use it again? How many types of mustard does one family need? Clean your refrigerator thoroughly. Now you're ready to load it up and get organized!

If you find that fruits and veggies often languish (and rot) in your refrigerator, place them at eye level so that the moment you open the door you'll be enticed to eat or prepare them. An overstuffed refrigerator can also contribute to this problem. Clear out leftovers quickly so you can easily view and assess the contents of your fridge.

Fridge Safety

According to the United States Department of Agriculture (USDA), refrigerators should keep food at 40°F or below. Place a refrigerator thermometer in your refrigerator to gauge the temperature. Hot food can be placed directly in the refrigerator or it can be rapidly chilled in an ice or cold water bath before refrigerating. A large pot of food like soup or stew should be divided into small portions and put in shallow containers before being refrigerated. A large cut of meat or whole poultry should be divided into smaller pieces or placed in shallow containers before refrigerating. Raw meat, poultry, and seafood should be in a sealed container or wrapped securely to prevent raw juices from contaminating other foods.

Good Storage

Cover foods to retain moisture and prevent them from picking up odors from other foods. Some refrigerators have special features such as adjustable shelves, door bins, crispers, and meat/cheese drawers. These features are designed to make storage of foods more convenient and to provide an optimal storage environment for fruits, vegetables, meats, poultry, and cheese. Stackable fridge trays can double your storage room by utilizing the full vertical space between shelves. Use square plastic containers for food storage, which allows easy stacking and conserves space.

In the Zone

Create zones in the fridge for different categories so you know where to find things. Put jams and jellies together on a shelf on the door and do the same for condiments. Keep your cheeses and meats together in the cheese drawer. Create one area that is for leftovers, another for beverages.

Tupperware makes storage containers called Forget Me Not, which are designed for leftover cheese, onions, and lemons. You place the food in the container and it hangs from a shelf so you can always find it.

Stay Organized

Always condense food down into smaller bowls and containers when you can. If your family uses a lot of beverages in cans, buy a can dispenser, which keeps them neatly organized. If you use many juice boxes, place them in a narrow storage box so they are together and don't fall over.

Try to store tall things in the back and short things in the front. Also, make an effort to store the things you use the least in the very back, or on the bottom shelf. Store foods in clear containers so that you can always know what is inside. Never place food in an open container in the fridge. It will spoil faster and affect the air quality inside the fridge. Keep veggies in plastic bags to preserve freshness. Try to space your items so that air can flow around them.

And keep the following tips in mind when deciding where to place refrigerated foods:

- **Don't get egg on your face:** Never keep eggs in the egg storage spot in the refrigerator door. This will expose them to air each time the door is opened and closed. Instead, keep them in the carton on an upper shelf in the refrigerator. The temperature of the storage bins in the door fluctuates more than the temperature in the cabinet.
- **Got milk:** Milk also does not belong in the door. Keep it on a tall shelf with other beverages.
- **Keep it crisp:** Crisper drawers are good for vegetables, such as peppers. These drawers typically have humidity controls designed to help prevent vegetables from losing moisture. (The drawers seal tightly, which limits oxygen intake. The more oxygen intake, the quicker a food will deteriorate and spoil.)
- **Watch your head:** Keep lettuce fresher by storing it unwashed in a heavy-duty zip-top bag. Discard the outer leaves that contain excess moisture. Wrap the lettuce in a paper towel, insert it in the plastic bag, squeeze as much air out of the bag as possible, and seal the bag.

Label all leftovers with a date so you know how long they've been hanging around. When you bring home the grocery shopping, rotate the items in your fridge, so the older carrots are in front of the newer ones, and so on. This way when people grab something, they will use the older items first. A refrigerator functions most efficiently when the air can circulate, so don't jam things in.

When you organize your refrigerator, don't just think in terms of making it functional. Think in terms of beauty as well. Fresh produce can be placed in attractive bowls in your refrigerator. If you encounter beauty each time you open your refrigerator door, you will have a natural incentive to keep it clean and to eat the foods that your body needs most.

Room-Temperature Items

Though you may be tempted to put all fresh foods in the fridge, this isn't a good idea for certain foods. For example, don't store potatoes in the refrigerator. The starch breaks down quickly, which leaves the potato mushy if baked. In the same way, tomatoes and cucumbers should be stored at room temperature. If you want these items cold in a salad, chill them before serving. Bananas, avocados, and zucchini should also be kept out.

Time It

Ever wondered how long you can keep milk past its sell-by date? Or sniffed some cold cuts and wondered if they were still safe to eat? Use this handy chart from the USDA to answer all your refrigerator food-storage questions:

STORAGE TIMES FOR REFRIGERATED FOODS	
Ground Meat, Ground Poultry, and Stew Meat	**Storage Time**
Ground beef, turkey, veal, pork, lamb	1–2 days
Stew meats	1–2 days
Fresh Meat (Beef, Veal, Lamb, and Pork)	**Storage Time**
Steaks, chops, roasts	3–5 days
Variety meats (tongue, kidneys, liver, heart, chitterlings)	1–2 days
Fresh Poultry	**Storage Time**
Chicken or turkey, whole	1–2 days
Chicken or turkey, parts	1–2 days
Giblets	1–2 days
Bacon and Sausage	**Storage Time**
Bacon	7 days
Sausage, raw from meat or poultry	1–2 days
Smoked breakfast links, patties	7 days
Summer sausage labeled "Keep Refrigerated"	unopened, 3 months; opened, 3 weeks
Hard sausage (such as pepperoni)	2–3 weeks
Ham, Corned Beef	**Storage Time**
Ham, canned, labeled "Keep Refrigerated"	unopened, 6–9 months; opened, 3–5 days
Ham, fully cooked, whole	7 days
Ham, fully cooked, half	3–5 days
Ham, fully cooked, slices	3–4 days

STORAGE TIMES FOR REFRIGERATED FOODS

Hot Dogs and Luncheon Meats	Storage Time
Hot dogs	unopened package, 2 weeks; opened package, 1 week
Luncheon meats	unopened package, 2 weeks; opened package, 3–5 days

Deli and Vacuum-Packed Products	Storage Time
Store-prepared (or homemade) egg, chicken, tuna, ham, and macaroni salads	3–5 days
Prestuffed pork, lamb chops, and chicken breasts	1 day
Store-cooked dinners and entrées	3–4 days
Commercial brand vacuum-packed dinners with USDA seal, unopened	2 weeks

Cooked Meat, Poultry, and Fish Leftovers	Storage Time
Pieces and cooked casseroles	3–4 days
Gravy and broth, patties, and nuggets	3–4 days
Soups and Stews	3–4 days

Fresh Fish and Shellfish	Storage Time
Fresh Fish and Shellfish	1–2 days

Eggs	Storage Time
Fresh, in shell	3–5 weeks
Raw yolks, whites	2–4 days
Hard-cooked	1 week
Liquid pasteurized eggs, egg substitutes	unopened, 10 days; opened, 3 days
Cooked egg dishes	3–4 days

Sell-By and Use-By

Some products have a "sell-by" date, while others have a "use-by" date. Understanding the difference can help you know when to keep something or toss it. The USDA defines the terms as follows:

- A "sell-by" date tells the store how long to display the product for sale. You should buy the product before the date expires. Products bought by the sell-by date will last as long as indicated in the chart earlier in this section. Additionally, according to the Dairy Council of California, with proper handling, milk should last 5 to 7 days after its sell-by date.
- A "best if used by (or before)" date is recommended for best flavor or quality. It is not a purchase or safety date.
- A "use-by" date is the last date recommended for the use of the product while at peak quality. The date has been determined by the manufacturer of the product. Use-by dates usually refer to best quality and are not safety dates. But even if the date expires during home storage, according to the USDA, a product should be safe, wholesome, and of good quality if handled properly and kept at 40°F or below.
- "Closed or coded" dates are packing numbers for use by the manufacturer and do not apply to you as a consumer, so ignore these.

If product has a use-by date, follow that date. If product has a sell-by date or no date, cook or freeze the product by the times on the chart in this chapter.

Inside and Out

When organizing your fridge, don't limit yourself to the inside. In many homes, refrigerators wind up becoming giant, messy canvases for magnet collages. Do your magnets multiply like rabbits? It might be handy to have the phone number of your favorite pizza delivery service, but you can put the refrigerator's magnetic properties to

If at some point you upgrade your kitchen, consider holding onto the old refrigerator and storing it in the basement or even the garage. It'll come in handy when you need the extra fridge space for entertaining or stocking up on sale items.

better use. Consolidate it all with a fridge door organizer, a vertical filing and dry-erase message center that can hold menus, homework, or coupons. Small magnetic shelves are a good idea for spices, paper towels, or hooks for utensils and potholders. But don't go overboard. Refrigerators dominate a kitchen and can get cluttered in no time.

Freezer Facts

Chest or upright freezers are a convenient way to store frozen food. Chest freezers are more energy efficient than uprights, while uprights make organization easier. If you have an extra stand-alone freezer, store it in the basement or the coolest part of your home. Then, if the power goes off, the ambient air temperature will keep the temperature inside the freezer cooler for a longer period of time.

There are several factors that affect the freezing process. Freezer food does not last forever and keeping things too long or storing them improperly can not only lead to food safety issues, but also impact flavor.

The USDA recommends setting your freezer for 0°F. Keep a freezer thermometer in your freezer to be sure the temperature is correct. If possible, turn your freezer to minus 10°F when you add food. When the food is frozen solid, you can turn the temperature back to 0°F. If you are opening your freezer often, it will not be able to maintain that temperature and foods will not last as long.

There are several factors in food that affect the freezing process. Here's a brief overview so you can get the most out of your freezer and this method of cooking.

To Freeze or Not to Freeze

Many foods freeze well. Meats, most vegetables, dairy products (including separated egg whites), fruits, sauces, combination dishes, breads, cakes, and casseroles will all hold their quality very well in the freezer and will reheat beautifully. Handling and preparation for storage will be the key.

Foods with a high-water content (lettuce, tomatoes, radishes) do not freeze well. All cells contain water, which expands when frozen. Cells of water-rich foods may break down too much as the water within them freezes, resulting in an unacceptable taste or soggy, mushy texture when thawed. Other foods that do not freeze well include:

- Whole hard-cooked eggs
- Raw eggs in the shell (remove from shell if you want to freeze and then use in cooking)
- Chopped or cut potatoes
- Celery
- Raw tomatoes
- Mayonnaise
- Custard and cream fillings
- Sour cream
- Cream sauces
- Fried foods
- Milk (it is safe to use, but the taste changes)
- Canned refrigerator dough

It's possible to work around some of these problem foods. Purchase already-frozen items, such as frozen potatoes; add them to the recipe after it has cooled; then immediately freeze the dish. When the recipe is thawed and reheated, the potatoes will be tender and perfect. Or you can also simply leave these foods out of the recipe when you're preparing it for the freezer, then add them during the thawing and reheating process.

Creamy dairy products can be frozen if a stabilizer is added to them, like flour or cornstarch. These items may separate when thawed, but a simple stir with a wire whisk will smooth out the sauce.

Freezer Times

Putting food in the freezer preserves it, but not forever. Frozen foods have a finite shelf life. Be on the safe side and label anything that's not on the menu in the upcoming week. You should try to freeze foods as fast as possible, which reduces the amount of ice crystals that form.

Consult the following list for the length of time specific foods will last in the freezer:

SAFE FREEZER–STORAGE TIMES	
Item	Months
Bacon and sausage	1 to 2
Casseroles	2 to 3
Egg whites or egg substitutes	12
Frozen dinners and entrées	3 to 4
Gravy, meat or poultry	3 to 4
Ham, hotdogs, and lunchmeats	1 to 2
Meat, uncooked roasts	4 to 12
Meat, uncooked steaks or chops	4 to 12
Meat, uncooked ground	3 to 4
Meat, cooked	2 to 3
Poultry, uncooked whole	12
Poultry, uncooked parts	9
Poultry, uncooked giblets	3 to 4
Poultry, cooked	4
Soups and stews	2 to 3
Wild game, uncooked	8 to 12

Bacteria and Molds

Bacteria and molds are present everywhere, even on the food we eat. Freezing does stop the growth of bacteria and mold on foods; however, when the food is thawed, these microorganisms will begin to grow again. That's why it is so important to thaw foods in the refrigerator instead of at room temperature.

Bacterial activity is still suppressed in the cold air of the fridge. Cooking destroys bacteria and molds, so it's very important to reheat frozen food properly and thoroughly before eating it.

Burn, Baby, Burn

A freezer is a hostile place. Foods that are not properly packaged for the freezer will become damaged very quickly. Freezer burn is the most common problem; it's simply the dehydration of food. When food is improperly wrapped, the dry environment of the freezer draws off moisture as the food freezes. This damages cells in the food and results in dry, hard patches that will not revert to the hydrated state even when thawed. Food that is affected by freezer burn is not unsafe to eat, but it will be tough and lack flavor. If only a small amount of food is affected, you can simply cut off that area and heat and eat the rest. If there is freezer burn over a large area of the food, however, throw it out; the taste and texture will be compromised.

Stews, soups, and other liquid foods that have been affected by freezer burn may be saved. These naturally liquid foods can absorb the damage caused by the dehydration when reheated. Slowly add small amounts of water to the dish when reheating, and stir gently, adding more as needed.

To prevent freezer burn, wrap foods tightly. Also be sure the supplies you purchase to wrap and store your food are specifically developed for the freezer environment, such as freezer plastic zip-top bags.

Enzymes and Oxidation

Enzymes that are naturally present in food cause changes in color, flavor, and texture. Enzymatic processes do not stop when food is frozen, although they do slow down. Some foods, particularly fruits and vegetables, need to be blanched or briefly cooked before freezing to disable these enzymes.

Cells are complete packages with membranes that control water and air exchange. When cells have been damaged (cut, chopped, or torn) by preparing or cooking the food, air combines with enzymes inside the cells. This process is called enzymatic oxidation, and it discolors food and changes flavors. Fats in meat can become rancid. The color of fruits and vegetables can become dull and drab. Freezing minimizes this process, and you can help by removing as much air as possible from the food when packaging it. Also, when you are preparing fruits for the freezer, coat the cut surfaces with an acidic liquid like lemon juice or an ascorbic acid solution to slow down the oxidation process.

Get the Air Out

Air is the enemy when you're freezing foods! Remove as much air as possible when wrapping. When you package food, press down on the container to get rid of excess air. You can use a drinking straw to draw air out before sealing the package. However, liquid items such as soups and stews need a small amount of space, called head space, in the container to allow for expansion during freezing. Leave ½" of head space in these containers so the lid doesn't pop off when the food expands as it freezes.

When adding new packages of food to your freezer, try to place them in the bottom of the freezer or against the sides. These are the coldest parts of the freezer, so the food will freeze more quickly without raising the internal temperature.

Freezer Zones

The freezer can be hard to keep organized—it's cold in there and you're usually getting in and out quickly! If you have an upright, designate specific shelves for specific types of foods, such as vegetables, meats, fish, prepared dishes, ice cream, and starches. If you have a chest freezer, make use of the baskets that came with it and consider adding some plastic storage boxes or crates to allow you to create the same zones.

Pack It Up

Proper packaging and wrapping will keep your food in excellent condition while it is being frozen and reheated. Make sure that there are no loose wrappings around the food.

The types of containers you use will determine how much food you'll be able to store in your freezer. Square and flat packages and containers make the best use of space, so you can add more packages to the freezer. Most casseroles can be frozen, removed from their dishes, and then stacked to store. To do this, line casserole and baking dishes with heavy-duty foil or freezer wrap. Freeze it. When the food is frozen solid, pop the food out of the dish, wrap again, and store. When you're ready to eat, simply place the frozen food back into the baking dish, thaw, and reheat.

Don't store tomato-based foods in foil; the acid in the tomatoes will eat through the foil, exposing the food to air and risking freezer burn. Use heavy-duty heatproof freezer wrap for these foods.

Freezers that are full are more efficient, so fill 'er up with sale items and bulk purchases. Bags of ice can help fill space as well. Adding too much to your freezer at once raises the temperature of the freezer and compromises the quality and safety of your stored food. Make sure that you never add the equivalent of more than 40 percent of your freezer space at one time. Be sure to refer to the manufacturer's instruction booklet for specifics for your type and size of freezer.

Do not store or freeze meat in its store packaging. Make sure breads are sealed inside plastic bags (not cellophane store bags which can rip when cold). Store soups and broths in zip-top bags and place them on a baking sheet on their sides so they freeze flat. You can then stack them. Frozen fruits and vegetables can be stored in the freezer as they come from the store. If you plan to keep ice cream for a long period of time, it is a good idea to seal it in plastic wrap or in a plastic bag or set the bag in a plastic container.

If you wish to store fresh herbs such as basil, store them in the freezer door in a plastic bag, or chop them in a food processor and freeze with a little water in an ice cube tray. Take out of the tray and store in zip-top bags. This is also a great way to freeze broth and puréed soups. Make sure you label and date all items.

There are some items you might not think of as freezer foods that can be stored very well in the freezer. Whole-wheat flour lasts longer in the freezer. (White flour, however, can be stored at room temperature.) Nuts and seeds can be stored in the freezer to prevent them from getting rancid. Freshly ground cornmeal lasts longer in the freezer.

You can cook foods right from the freezer, but they will take about one and a half times as long to cook compared to defrosted foods.

Get Ready for the Deep Freeze

Food you've prepared has to be properly packed, wrapped, and frozen to preserve it in the best possible quality. Do not place hot foods in your freezer. Before placing the food in your freezer, cool it as quickly as you can. Hot foods will raise the temperature of your freezer and could compromise the safety and quality of other foods stored there. When the food has been prepared as the recipe directs, place it in a metal cooking or baking pan, in an ice-water bath, or spread the food in a shallow pan and place it in the refrigerator for thirty to fifty minutes. Then pack the food in the freezer containers or wrap, seal, label, and freeze immediately.

In a Flash

Flash freezing is simply freezing foods as quickly as possible. Individual appetizers, sandwiches, rolls, cookies, and other small-size foods retain their quality, shape, and form best when flash frozen. Spread a layer of food on a cookie sheet or another flat surface and freeze individually—leave a space of ½ to 1" between the individual pieces of food so cold air can circulate freely—then package in one container once frozen solid. Flash freezing also allows you to freeze things like berries or shrimp and then place them all in a bag together and not have them freeze in a giant lump. The items will stay separate.

Use freezer tape to seal seams when you use freezer wrap to package food. Buy erasable, reusable labels for your food-storage containers.

Meat Market

There are very specific rules you need to follow when purchasing and storing large quantities of meat. Most important, pay attention to expiration dates on meat products and never buy or freeze meat that is past those dates. Do not freeze meat in its original packaging. Wrap it in freezer wrap, heavy-duty foil, or zip-top freezer bags; label and freeze. Divide the meat into small quantities before you package it for refreezing so it will be easier to thaw and work with. Freeze chicken parts or fish fillets separately, and then combine in a larger bag. Pork chops should be separated by freezer wrap, then combined in a larger bag or wrapped together with freezer wrap. Large quantities of ground beef should be divided into thin portions (patties) and packaged divided by parchment or freezer paper. Do the same with other ground meats.

Checklist

Just as you did with the pantry, you should create a list of everything in your freezer. Cross items off when you use them and add things to the list when you buy them. Keep the list on top of an upright freezer or attached with a magnet to the front or side of a chest freezer.

Defrosting

Most refrigerator/freezer combos sold today don't require defrosting. A few combo units that do require defrosting are still sold and you may have an old one in your home. If you own one, frost will build up in the freezer compartment and you need to defrost it periodically. Most stand-alone chest or upright freezers that are sold today require defrosting.

When food is removed from the freezer for defrosting and the unit is turned off, it's important to keep refrigerated foods cold and frozen foods from thawing. Place the food in a cooler with a cold source or pack it in a box and cover it with blankets for insulation. Place frozen ice packs or bags of ice cubes on top of the food. The food will be safe to refreeze as long as it is still frozen solid.

While defrosting your freezer, discard packages that are more than a year old and store the remaining frozen items in an insulated ice chest.

It is not safe to use an ice pick, knife, or anything sharp to remove the ice. Instead, you just need to let it melt. The USDA says it is not safe to use any electrical heating device in or near the freezer to defrost it. Instead, just leave the door open and it will defrost on its own.

To defrost food from the freezer there are only three safe methods: in the refrigerator, in cold water (changing the water every thirty minutes), or in the microwave. It is not safe to allow food to sit out to defrost. If you have defrosted the food in the refrigerator but have not cooked it, it is safe to refreeze. Cooked foods can be refrozen as well. Leftovers should be frozen within three to four days.

If you have a power outage, your full freezer of food is good for two days if you keep the door closed. If it is not full, rearrange the foods so they are grouped together and will last longer. If the food is 40°F (for up to two hours) when the power comes back on, it is safe to refreeze. Putting your frozen food outside in cold weather is not recommended since the sun can defrost it even if it is cold out.

Kitchen **CLEANUP**

8

Cleaning and organizing are closely related. It's difficult to clean until you've reduced your clutter. After you've organized, cleaning brings that final polish to your kitchen and it's easier to keep a clean kitchen clutter-free. Just as you've had to develop organizational strategies that will work over the long haul, you'll also want to develop cleaning strategies that are simple and effective and will work for years to come. This chapter will offer cleaning tips—from speed cleaning to green cleaning and everything in between—that will help you tackle every cleaning job in your kitchen.

Expect Imperfection

Perfectionism can be paralyzing, just as a willingness to embrace imperfection can be liberating. Cleaning is always a work in progress because life in the kitchen is messy—the more people and animals that share a space, and the more activities you do in that space, the messier it becomes. One of the best ways to adapt yourself to this reality is to expect that you probably won't be able to achieve constant perfection on every front all the time.

Once you've been able to relax into this reality, you'll be better able to develop cleaning systems that will be adaptable to a variety of circumstances. You might want to think in terms of developing weekly and daily rituals. The FlyLady recommends that certain tasks be delegated to specific days—for example, you could plan to wash the floor on Friday, dust the shelves on Saturday, and wipe down all the appliances Monday. This type of system can keep you from feeling overwhelmed, because you simply focus on the task that you've planned to do on a single day instead of feeling swamped by undone tasks and worrying about how to manage them all. This kind of system might also allow you to keep your kitchen more consistently clean because you'll be rotating through the major weekly tasks instead of procrastinating for weeks on end on the projects that you find least desirable.

Whatever kind of cleaning system you adopt, allow for flexibility. Allow yourself to fail without becoming overly critical. Most people were never really taught to clean well—this is a skill that can be learned with time, patience, and persistence. Different phases of your life will place different demands on you, and sometimes you'll find yourself in a messier kitchen. Just be realistic about what is possible within the confines of your own life, pace yourself, and continue to take steps toward your goals. Know that you'll surely hit obstacles along the way, but if you're not too daunted by imperfection, you'll be able to overcome them.

Small Steps

Although cleaning is often thought of as a chore, it can be simplified, and in some cases even enjoyed, if you find a deeper meaning in the work. The more you strategize about cleaning solutions that will work for you, the more likely you are to feel involved in and challenged by the process. Cleaning does not just have to be about the final product, but the actual process can be good for you—cleansing your mind and giving you a break from the more abstract work that might be associated with your job. And remember, if you continue to take small steps each day to order your home and to make it beautiful, that feeling of peace and contentment will grow until it permeates the entire house.

One of the best ways to increase your cleaning efficiency (and your efficiency in almost any area of life) is to find ways to enjoy the task. If you can find ways to transform kitchen cleaning from a chore into a game, you're halfway there.

Speed Cleaning

If you want to reduce dramatically the amount of time you spend cleaning, try speed cleaning. It will help you not only spend less time cleaning, but also to spend less money on cleaning products.

- Work from the top down. Because gravity pulls dirt and debris downward, it makes no sense to clean the floor before cleaning the counter.
- If it's clean, skip it! There's nothing that says everything must be cleaned on a certain schedule; so if it's not dirty, don't waste time.
- Speed is the word. Your goal is to move as quickly as possible through the house, and lingering will slow you down.
- Use the right tools for the right jobs. In some cases, you'll need to invest in heavier-duty tools to tackle tougher jobs. Keep all cleaning tools and supplies in good shape so that you won't waste time on leaky bottles, broken brooms, and vacuums that have lost their ability to pick up dirt effectively.
- Put all cleaning items away in the proper place when you're done. Otherwise, you'll lose time hunting for them.
- Pay attention to the amount of time it takes to speed clean your home and strive to get a little faster each time.
- Use both of your hands and you'll dramatically increase your speed. Finish one step with one hand and start the next job with the other.

With cleaning, there are many shortcuts you can take. Be creative about developing your own strategies for making the work fun and efficient.

Race Against the Clock

Many people feel that this kind of game can make cleaning much more enjoyable and manageable. If you know you're going to set the timer and only clean for a designated amount of time, you're less likely to feel overwhelmed by the scope of the task. It is always easier to take on a five-minute project than it is to attempt to tackle a two-hour one. Another benefit of transforming cleaning into a game is that it is much easier to get children involved in a fun game or race than it is to try to get them involved in household "work."

Kids, Too!

If you're tired of cleaning up after your kids, challenge them to join in. Visit any well-run preschool room and you'll see many ways that teachers integrate the work of cleaning into the school day. In some preschools, children sing a song as they clean. In others, children are just reminded to clean up after themselves after meals and snacks. While kids may balk at these kinds of directives at home, they generally obey their teachers because they understand from the beginning that cleaning is part of the arrangement.

If you want to make cleanup fun for your children, there are a few things to keep in mind. First, just as you need not (and should not) demand perfection from yourself in the domestic realm, don't expect perfection from your kids. Think of every cleaning effort on their part as "training" for them. If you encourage and point out the good work they're doing, they'll be more inclined to keep going. If you criticize and correct, they're likely to become discouraged and quit. Either ignore their failings so that they can develop a long-term positive association with cleaning or offer suggestions in an encouraging way, such as, "You're doing a great job washing the pots. Would you like me to show you how I wash glasses?"

> Clean up spilled oil by sprinkling it with flour, letting it absorb, then sweeping it up.

You can also get really creative with children and cleaning. Try making sock puppets for dusting and have a contest to see who can pick up the most dirt in a set amount of time. Or put on a CD and every time a song ends, switch to the next chore. It's also a good idea to invest in kid-sized cleaning implements when children are small so that they can mimic you as you sweep, vacuum, and dust. This way, cleaning might feel less intimidating to them as they grow older.

Checking off a List

Some people work better if they have a checklist to go through. Create a checklist for yourself or use this one. Working through the checklist lets you see what you've done and still need to do.

Cleaning Checklist

Daily

___ Wipe kitchen table and chairs with damp cloth.

___ Wipe counters with damp cloth.

___ Rinse sink.

___ Wipe stovetop with damp cloth.

___ Wash dishes.

___ Wipe nonwashable placemats with damp cloth.

Weekly

___ Clean stovetop with cleaner.

___ Clean countertops with cleaner.

___ Clean sink with cleaner.

___ Clean dishwasher.

___ Wipe cabinets.

___ Shake out or vacuum rugs and mats.

___ Sweep and mop floor.

___ Clean baseboards and kick plates.

___ Clean small appliances.

___ Clean outsides of dishwasher, refrigerator, and oven.

___ Clean garbage disposal.

___ Dust display items.

___ Clean tabletop with cleaner.

___ Dust window sills.

___ Wash placemats.

___ Empty trash.

See the section later in this chapter called "Spring Is in the Air" for a spring cleaning list for jobs to be done a few times per year.

Warning: According to *www.webmd.com*, the kitchen sponge is the number one source of germs in your entire house. The site recommends placing your damp sponge in the microwave for two minutes on high to kill all germs. Replace dishrags once a week and allow them to completely dry between uses.

Green Cleaning

Increasingly, people are searching for cleaning methods that are safe, cheap, and efficient. During pregnancy, especially, many women cannot tolerate the smell of many of the more toxic cleaners, such as bleach and oven cleaners. Although limited exposure to household cleaners may not cause harm to human health, nobody knows for sure what the threshold is. At what point do household cleaners become a threat to those who live in a home? Some studies suggest that certain people—such as children and the elderly—are more vulnerable to negative health impacts from household cleaners than are more resilient groups.

Warning: If you use conventional house cleansers, never mix products— especially products containing bleach. Some people have actually died from the fumes created by accidental toxic blends. Also be sure to rinse well between products to prevent them from mingling. Be mindful as well, that although ammonia is a common cleaner, when it is combined with bleach, it becomes toxic. Never mix bleach with any chemical or "natural" cleaner.

If you clean the inside of your home with nontoxic products, you and your family might become healthier as well. The United States Environmental Protection Agency has determined that, in many homes, levels of indoor pollution can be somewhere between two to five times higher than outdoor pollutants. Surprisingly, newer homes (those built after 1970) are at a greater risk for this problem because these homes tend to be better sealed against the elements than older homes. While these homes are generally more heat efficient than their older counterparts, the tight seal on the windows and doors also prevents household toxins—not just those from cleansers, but also carbon monoxide from gas appliances—from escaping.

Green Choices

While organic foods typically cost more than conventional foods, this trend generally does not carry over into cleaning products. While purchasing ready-made natural cleaners at a health-food store may be more expensive than purchasing cleaning products at your local drugstore, there are many simple household items that are cheap to stock, easy to work with, and nontoxic. These items, which most people already have on hand, can assist you as you begin to explore green cleaning.

Baking soda is a cheap, environmentally friendly alternative to harsher cleaners. It is so safe that you can not only use it on your teeth and in baking, but you can also use it to scour tiles, remove the grime from sinks, get rid of odors in the refrigerator and on carpets, and wipe down your kitchen counters. Using this as a cleaner makes getting organized for cleaning a snap because you will most likely always have baking soda in your cupboard. Even if you prefer to use other cleaners, this is a great backup cleaner in a pinch because you'll have it at the ready.

Not only are these ordinary household items cheaper than conventional household cleaners, it can be fun to play the chemist by mixing up your own green cleaners. A small amount of lavender oil or lemon can bring a fresh aroma to many areas. Experiment with these products until you find combinations that work for your home.

Here is a list of green-cleaning products, as well as possible uses for each of them.

- **Olive oil:** Mix three parts oil to one part vinegar to clean wooden cabinets and table and chairs.
- **Club soda:** Use for windows and chrome.
- **Coffee:** Place the grounds in old pantyhose and use as a scrubber.
- **Vinegar:** Perfect for cleaning hardwood floors and also good for cutting grime, soap buildup, and for mold.
- **Borax:** Can kill mold and disinfect.
- **Salt:** When mixed with water, can kill bacteria; make a paste of it for scrubbing tough grime.
- **Lemons:** Run them through your garbage disposal for a fresh clean scent.
- **Baking soda:** Can be used to scour and remove odors, and can be combined with vinegar to clean stainless steel.

Give Yourself a Hand

As you become more realistic with yourself about your skills and capacities, consider hiring a cleaning person. This hiring does not have to be a substantial investment. You could hire a cleaning person to come just once a month, for example, or every other week. Even if you are on a tight budget, a cleaning person might still be in your budget if you can find ways to reduce your overall spending.

The cost of hiring a professional cleaning person varies a great deal depending on where you live. In a rural area, where the cost of living is generally lower than a larger city, you can expect to pay less than in a major urban area. Think of hiring a cleaning person to come in and do the really tough jobs, like cleaning your oven (if it is not self-cleaning), or washing the windows.

The Kitchen Sink and Everything under It

Open up your under-sink cabinets and you'll probably find all sorts of things, including cleaning supplies you've forgotten. It's hard to resist sampling a new product when the manufacturer promises its newest glass cleaner, stainless-steel polisher, lemon oil, or detergent will make your life easier. But are they all necessary? Imagine how much space you could free up if just a handful of cleaners served multiple functions. There are a few multitasking products on the market. A product called Holy Cow (*www.holycowproducts.com*), for instance, can clean your walls, grout, and granite, and even your jewelry and shoe leather. Pare down your cleaning supplies so that the items you do have can multitask, saving you space.

The spot under your sink is a valuable storage space that you should maximize. Take advantage of the space by investing in adjustable-height shelving that slides out along rails and is specially designed to fit around awkward drain pipes.

Another way to organize all those cleaners, brushes, and sponges is to buy a tool caddy. Fill it with the cleaners you use most often, then when you're cleaning, you can just grab the caddy and have everything you need with you in a handy container. Install some hooks on the wall or door under the sink to hang brushes.

Warning: Some of the household products stored under your sink may be toxic and fall under the classification of hazardous waste. Don't pour them down the drain or throw them in the trash. Contact the appropriate environmental agency for your area or call your town hall to find out how to dispose of chemical cleaners properly and safely.

Ending the Science Experiment

The refrigerator and freezer are two of the hardest spots in the kitchen to clean. They're never empty and it's challenging to reach every spot. Wipe the outside of the fridge and freezer (and the handles) weekly, and check expiration dates on food. Clean the inside of your fridge and freezer every few months.

The first step in cleaning your refrigerator is to empty it out and clean it. Remove all of the shelves and clean them. If you have glass or plastic shelves, try using a natural cleaner (such as baking soda) without harmful chemicals. Because the refrigerator is a contained and well-sealed space, you don't want chemicals compromising the indoor air quality—or leaving residue on your apples and blueberries. Take out the drawers and wash them in the sink with a mild cleaner, or with baking soda and water. Dry them thoroughly. Wipe down the walls of the refrigerator with your natural cleaner. Clean inside the butter compartment and all of the shelves on the door. Wipe down the seal around the door.

Clean out the coils underneath the refrigerator. They get coated with dust and pet fur and work less efficiently. Pull out the refrigerator and vacuum or sweep behind it. Wipe down the back and sides of the refrigerator with a damp cloth. The front of the refrigerator should be cleaned with a mild or natural cleaner. If you have a stainless-steel refrigerator, purchase a stainless-steel cleaner.

Water and ice dispensers can become coated with hard-water buildup. To clean these, use Lime-A-Way or vinegar. You may need to fill a glass with some of the diluted cleaner and hold it up so the water and ice dispensers can soak in the glass for a few minutes. The hard-water residue will wipe right off after being soaked.

To clean the freezer, you need to unload it and defrost it. Clean shelves, drawers, and walls as you did in the refrigerator, and wipe down the seal around the door. Empty the ice bin and wash it in the sink.

Feel the Heat

The stove and oven can be one of the dirtiest spots in your kitchen. Keeping this area clean will help your kitchen seem neater. To make cleaning easier, always try to wipe up spills as soon as they happen. If they get cooked on, they are much harder to remove.

Start with the stovetop. Unplug the stove if you are dealing with an electric stove. If you have a stove with burners, remove all the grates and drip pans.

Soak these in a mixture of hot water and baking soda or a multipurpose cleaner mixed with water. Remove the knobs and clean them with the same mixture. If you have an electric stove, you should not soak the burners in water. To clean them, wipe them with a damp cloth soaked in a water and vinegar mix; then rinse. If there are any hard to remove spots, make a paste of baking soda and water and allow it to rest for a few hours. A Mr. Clean Magic Eraser is another cleaning option.

To clean the stovetop, use baking soda or an all-purpose cleaner. Allow it to soak on grimy spots before wiping away. If you're stuck with dirt you just can't get off, spray it with a little oven cleaner and let it soak, then wipe it off. Glass stovetops can present a challenge, because they always look streaky. Clean with baking soda or a glass-stovetop cleaner. Polish with a vinegar and water solution.

Most ovens are self-cleaning these days, but if yours is not, pour salt on any spills as soon as they happen. Scrub it out when cool. If anything remains, clean it with a paste of baking soda and water. Clean the walls and shelves of the oven with baking soda and water. You can also purchase a spray-on oven cleaner, but be careful not to breathe the fumes in. It's tempting to want to put foil on the bottom of the oven to allow for easy cleanup, but it impacts the movement of heat and is not a good idea.

Tackling the Sink

If you have a stainless-steel sink, wipe it out with vinegar and water, or a multipurpose cleaner. Scrub any spots with vinegar and water or cleaners like Bar Keepers Friend. If you want the steel to shine, rub it with a little vegetable or olive oil when you're done.

Porcelain, enameled metal, and solid surface sinks can be difficult to clean because you can't use abrasive cleaners. Wipe out the sink with a vinegar and water solution. You can rub a cut lemon on any stains to fade them. A bleach pen can be used on a white porcelain sink for very tough spots. Solid-surface sinks like Corian can be rubbed with a green scrubbing pad to rub away the stain.

Counters and Cabinets

Your counters and cabinets are the areas of your kitchen that are most easily seen. If you keep these clean and shiny, your whole kitchen will feel cleaner. To clean your countertop, take everything off it. Wipe up all crumbs and dirt. Spray the countertop with a vinegar and water solution, or a mixture of water and mild soap. Wipe it off. Scrub any sticky spots. Be sure to get under the edge of the counter and the backsplash, as well as in any seams.

If you have wood cabinets, you'll want to use a wood cleaner. There is a special cleaner just for cabinets called Cabinet Magic that works well. Be sure to clean all drawer pulls and handles with mild soap.

Getting Down to It

If you have area rugs, vacuum them or shake them out first, then take them out of the room so you can clean beneath them. For a thorough job, turn the kitchen chairs upside down on the table to give you full access to the floor. Pick up any baskets, bowls, or plants on the floor.

Sweep the floor with a broom and dustpan to get the loose dirt cleaned up. You can also use a vacuum, but be sure to put it on the "no carpet" setting to stop the brushes from spinning and shooting the dirt around the room.

If you have tile, the grout is probably your biggest challenge. To do a thorough job, you'll want to scrub the grout with a toothbrush or other small brush. Use grout cleaner, baking soda, or for very tough stains on white grout, a bleach pen.

Once you've got the grout scrubbed, mop the floor with an all-purpose cleaner diluted in a bucket. A mop you can wring out is essential, and you may want to follow the mop with a towel (put it under one foot and run it over the floor) to get the floor very clean and dry. This same procedure works to clean a linoleum or vinyl floor.

If you have a wood floor in your kitchen, clean it with a wood floor cleaner. After mopping the floors, take a damp cloth and wipe down the baseboards and kick plates of the room.

Little 'Lectrics

Small appliances get sticky and smudged. To get them completely clean, first unplug them; then take apart pieces like bowls on food processors so you can thoroughly clean the entire surface of the machine. Wipe the outside down with a cloth that is dampened with an all-purpose cleaner and water mixture, or water and vinegar. For tough dirt, spray the cleaner directly on the dirt, or scrub with a mix of baking soda and water. Dry with a clean cloth. Remember to wipe down the electrical cord, since this often gets sticky and dirty too.

Empty out the crumb tray on toasters and toaster ovens. Clean the glass on a toaster oven with window cleaner or vinegar and water. The working parts and accessories of food processors, blenders, and mixers should be washed in soap and water if they are dirty. When cleaning a can opener, lift the handle and clean the entire mechanism thoroughly. Use a baking soda paste on any caked-on grime.

To clean the inside of the microwave, first place a glass measuring cup half filled with water in it and run on high for three minutes. The steam will loosen all the dirt. Remove the tray and wash with dish soap. Wipe down the inside with a baking soda and water mixture. You don't want harsh chemicals inside this space where you cook food. Tired of things spattering all over the microwave? Buy a plastic microwave-safe lid that will fit over just about any size dish or bowl in the microwave to contain explosions.

Enlightenment

Keep your kitchen bright and cheery by keeping your light fixtures clean. Clean them every few months. Turn the light off and remove the bulb to allow you easy access to the entire fixture. If you have a fixture with a screw-on glass cover, carefully remove it and place it on a towel and clean it there. Spray with glass cleaner (or vinegar and water) and wipe until smudge-free.

Ceiling fans can get incredibly dirty (puzzling, since they're constantly in motion). Clean these every few months. Make sure the switch is set to *off*. Carefully climb up a step stool or stepladder (have someone spot you if necessary). Use a cloth dampened in an all-purpose cleaner to wipe the top, bottom, and sides of the blade. Also wipe the covering of the fan mechanism and any chains or cords that hang down.

Table and Chairs

Keep your eating area clean and crumb-free so that you enjoy the space for eating and also for the many other activities that tend to happen here. Wipe the tabletop after each meal with a damp cloth. Wipe crumbs off the seats of the chairs. Once a week, clean a wooden table and chairs with a wood cleaner. If you have cushions on your chairs, shake them out every few days. Spot-clean stains with Shout Wipes. Wash your placemats once a week. If they are not washable, wipe them off with a soapy cloth several times a week.

Plastic and wooden high chairs can be hard to get clean. If you have a plastic high chair, it can be put in the shower and scrubbed and sprayed there. Using the hose outside is also a great solution. Clean wooden high chairs with a wood cleaner like Murphy's Oil Soap. The tray on any high chair should be cleaned after each use.

Dishwasher Details

Researchers at the University of Bonn in Germany determined that using a dishwasher cleaned the dishes better and saved energy and time over doing the dishes by hand. If you are using a dishwasher, you do not need to rinse your dishes. Modern dishwashers are able to clean any dishes, as long as larger pieces of food are removed.

- Load the plates in the bottom rack, facing towards the center.
- Pots can be placed face down on this rack.
- Flat pans, cutting boards, and baking sheets can be placed in upright; they usually fit best along the outside edges.
- Glasses and cups go on the top rack, spaced so they are not touching each other.

- Place bowls and saucers down the center section of the top rack, at an angle.
- Plastic containers and items should also go on the top, so they are far away from the heating element.
- Silverware and utensils go in the silverware basket. If you'll be washing both silver and stainless-steel flatware in the dishwasher, don't put them in the same basket section. You want to avoid allowing one metal to touch the other. Alternate the direction of the silverware—some should have the handle up and some should have it down so that you don't end with spoons "spooning," making it impossible for them to get clean.
- Utensils such as spatulas and cooking spoons should be placed handle down.
- Fill the soap holder and also be sure to fill the spot for the rinse agent regularly. Jet Dry or just plain white vinegar will keep your glassware spot- and streak-free.

Since the dishwasher cleans your dishes and is constantly running with soapy water you might think you don't need to clean it, but actually regular cleaning will help it last longer. To clean the outside, wipe with glass cleaner or all-purpose cleaner. If your dishwasher is stainless steel, use a stainless steel-cleaner.

Once a month, pull the racks out and scrub any areas of grime or crusted-on goop (this often accumulates around the wheels). Clean the silverware basket. Wipe around the seals of the door and empty out any basket at the bottom that catches food scraps. If you see any areas inside the dishwasher that are discolored, scrub them with baking soda. Run the dishwasher empty on high temperature, heated dry, with soap, after you do this.

Dishpan Hands

There is an American proverb that says, "Wishes won't wash dishes." If washing the dishes is one of your most dreaded chores, take heart! There are ways to simplify and streamline the process. One great tip is to fill your sink with soapy water while you're cooking. Then just place your dirty dishes and pots and pans in the sink to soak as you continue cooking. When you're ready to do the dishes, they'll be half done already. Another easy cleanup tip is to rinse your utensils, pots, and cutting boards as you're cooking, then reuse them for the next task. Dishes won't stack up.

To do your dishes by hand, use two sinks: one with hot, soapy water to wash and one filled with cooler water to rinse. If you don't have two sinks, place a rubber bin inside your sink and use that for washing and then rinse in the remaining part of the sink.

- Start with the glasses, so they are washed in the cleanest water. It is best to dry your glasses with a linen towel to remove all streaks and water spots.
- Next, wash your plates with a sponge, soft brush, or dishtowel. As you are washing the plates, place your silverware in the bottom of the sink. It will soak and be easy to just rinse by the time you get to it.
- Get those pieces of silverware done next, being sure that the spaces between the tines of the forks are clean.
- Do the serving dishes next.
- Wash utensils next.
- Save the pots and pans for last. Very greasy or baked-on food should be soaked for at least a few hours and adding baking soda to the water can help. Dawn Power Dissolver is a product that helps remove baked-on stains. If you have cooked-on food in a pot, fill it partway with water and put it on the stove to boil. The boiling water will loosen the dirt.
- If you are washing very breakable items, line the bottom of the sink with a towel to protect them.

Odds and Ends

There are many other little things in the kitchen that can use a good cleaning now and again. Be sure to clean out the inside of your garbage can every few months. Take it outside and spray it with a hose if you can. The fruit bowl needs to be washed once a week. Wipe down your salt and pepper shakers and things like olive oil bottles and soap dispensers once a week. Clean doorknobs, window latches, and all handles and pulls in the room with an all-purpose cleaner. Wipe down your telephone completely. Wash your spoon rest in soapy water. Go around the perimeter of the room with a feather duster, or with a rag on the end of a mop and get rid of the cobwebs that accumulate along the walls.

Eliminate Pests

No one wants to see roaches scurrying or ants marching across the kitchen counters or down the walls. But before using pesticides, people can consider other alternatives available to control pests.

One of the first steps to reducing pests and insects in the house is removing whatever it is that is attracting them. Keep counters and floors clean of food scraps. And dripping faucets and soaking dishes should be avoided because they serve as a water source enticing insects into the kitchen. Keep foods that pests find attractive such as flour, macaroni, and cornmeal in tightly closed containers to eliminate easy access by bugs.

There are natural ways to rid your kitchen of some of the more common pests without using pesticides. Follow a trail of ants to find where they are coming in. Sprinkle chili pepper, dried peppermint, or borax to steer them away. For cockroaches mix borax, sugar, and flour and sprinkle it in the infested area. Also try sprinkling borax behind light switches, under sinks, and in the back of cabinets to kill roaches.

Spring Is in the Air

It's called spring cleaning, but you really can do it at any time of the year. A spring cleaning is a deep cleaning, where you clean nooks and crannies you normally might not get to. For a complete kitchen spring cleaning, make sure you do the following:

- Pull out your stove and fridge to clean underneath and behind them.
- Wash curtains or wipe down blinds.

- Turn the chairs upside down and wipe off the glides on the feet of the chairs.
- Wipe the table legs and chair legs with wood cleaner.
- If your table takes a leaf, pop it open and clean out the crack where the leaf fits—it gets packed with dirt and crumbs.
- Wipe out window sills.
- Clean the outsides of the windows.
- Wash screens on windows.
- Empty out the pantry, cupboards, and drawers and wipe them clean.
- Thoroughly dust all display items in the kitchen.
- Wash out the soap dispenser.
- Clean light fixtures and fans.
- Clean light switches.
- Replace your kitchen scrub brush and sponges.
- Wash all washable rugs and mats.
- Dust the top of the refrigerator.
- Wipe down the sides of flower and plant pots.
- Use a damp cloth to wipe the inside and outside of all baskets.

Flamed

If you have a grill, no matter how humble, you have an outdoor kitchen. Your grill needs to be cleaned just like your stove. You may want to place your grill on a grill pad to prevent grease drips on your patio or deck.

Charcoal Grills

Clean the grate before each use with a wire brush or crumpled piece of foil. Scoop out any ashes from the bottom. Empty out the entire grill at least once a year and rinse it out. Use a brush to scrub any caked-on grease and use a steel wool pad for tough spots.

Gas Grills

Clean the grate before each use with a wire brush or crumpled piece of foil. Once a year disengage the gas and scrub down the inside of the lids and the inside of the cooking area with an all-purpose cleaner or a steel wool pad. Change the briquettes. Empty or replace the grease catcher as needed. If the grill is rusting, it needs to be painted. Check the connectors to the propane tank for any cracks or problems.

Tools

Clean your grill tools after each use with hot, soapy water. Include things like fish baskets, grill trays, and pans, as well as your fork, spatula, and tongs.

On Stage

If you're trying to sell your home, your kitchen is a prime-selling point. Staging is a process that allows you to emphasize the room's highlights to a potential buyer. The first step is doing a very thorough cleaning of the room. Make it shine. Then:

- Get everything completely organized, down to having mug handles facing the same way and cereal boxes lined up according to height (doing so will convince the buyer you are overly meticulous and take incredible care of your entire home).
- Put away all scrub brushes, dish rags, and dish soap so the sink area looks spacious and empty.
- Put a little vanilla on a baking sheet and place it on the oven on warm for about half an hour before anyone comes to view the home. The smell will be inviting.
- Remove anything that is blocking your windows (such as sun catchers or hanging plants). You want the room to feel bright and airy.
- Unload the dishwasher before anyone comes in case buyers open it (and they often do).

- Clean out your drawers and cupboards because people will look inside them. You want them to look roomy and large, not small and cramped with tons of stuff.
- Stash away all small countertop appliances (like can openers and food processors) so the counter looks bigger and the room feels more spacious.

There are some inexpensive changes that will make the room look terrific, such as replacing drawer pulls and handles, bringing in new area rugs, replacing drip trays on the stove, placing a plant on the counter, and touching up the paint in the room. If you don't have room in your kitchen for a full-size kitchen table, consider buying a small two-person table with chairs to make the room look as if it does have an eating area.

Set your kitchen table with beautiful table settings, cloth napkins, nice glassware, and a lovely centerpiece. If you don't have dishes nice enough to set the table, place a bowl of fresh fruit in the center of the table.

Depersonalize the room by putting away photos, lists, calendars, and anything that reminds a buyer that someone else uses this kitchen. Take out the trash before buyers arrive, and consider removing the trash can completely while the home is being shown. If you have pets, stash their dishes, toys, leashes, and litter boxes. Buyers don't need visual notice that an animal lives in the home.

PART 3　COOKING, SHOPPING, AND MEAL PLANNING

9

Read BETWEEN the Lines

If you enjoy cooking, chances are, over time you'll acquire many recipes in many different forms—from cookbooks and magazine clippings, to printouts from the Internet and handwritten notes from friends and family. Keeping those recipes organized and easy to use takes a little planning. You'll learn how in this chapter. You may also be wondering how to find new recipes and cooking ideas easily, and this chapter will discuss that as well. The more accessible and usable your recipes are, the more likely you will be to try new things and expand your food horizons.

Carded

One of the most traditional ways to store and organize recipes is through recipe cards; index-sized cards stored in a little metal, plastic, or wooden box. Your grandma probably had one. The fun thing about recipe cards is they can be personalized so easily. You can buy all sorts of fun designs, both in cards and in boxes. Recipe cards are also easy to use because you just pull out the one you need and put it on the counter as you cook. You can buy cute, themed recipe card holders which will keep your card upright while you are cooking.

Recipe cards have some drawbacks though. Very long recipes don't fit on the cards, requiring you to staple or paperclip two together. Most recipes don't even fit on the front of the card, so you're constantly flipping the card over to read ingredients and instructions. If you cut a recipe out of a magazine or print it out online, it won't fit on the card. And the cards get dirty and stain easily. (There is a solution to the last problem. Buy clear, plastic index-card sleeves and slip them over each recipe.)

Recipe Notebooks

A recipe notebook allows you to fit an entire recipe on one page. You could use a spiral notebook, or a composition notebook (and both of these come in a wide range of colors and styles). Choose one with a plastic cover to give it a long life. You can write recipes in the notebook, or paste in recipes from magazines or the web. The notebook is very portable and fits nicely on a shelf with your cookbooks.

The biggest problem with the notebook system is you can't easily move recipes around, which means you can't organize them. They stay in the notebook in the order in which you added them, which can make it challenging to find that recipe for stuffed mushrooms you remember adding last year. The pages are also susceptible to stains and smudges. Many of these problems can be solved by using recipe binders.

Recipe Binders

Three-ring binders offer a great system, particularly if you have a large number of recipes. Use dividers to create sections like "Appetizers," "Desserts," "Chicken Dishes," and so on. If you have a lot of recipes, you may want to break them up among several binders. Buy different colors so it is easy to know which one to grab. The binders that lock last the longest.

Buy a box of clear-plastic page protectors and slide two recipes in each (one facing each direction), so your recipes won't get stained as you cook. This system is convenient because it allows you to move recipes around, add new ones, and you can simply open the binder and pull out the recipe you need. It's also convenient for sharing recipes, because you can photocopy, scan, or fax a recipe easily. The binders store well with your cookbooks.

Another storage option is to use color-coded files to store different categories of recipes. You can store the files in a file cabinet, or in a kitchen drawer or cabinet. The files are easy to grab and easy to add to, but are hard to keep organized and clean. However, these can work if you don't have room for bulky binders.

Go Digital

"There's an app for that." Recipes can now be easily organized and managed digitally, through your computer, tablet, or smartphone. Scan or type in your hard copy recipes to create a digital-cookbook document you can search and easily manipulate. Save it as a PDF download to your tablet or e-book reader. You can also synch your smartphone and open it there. You can upload digital-cookbook documents to Apple's iCloud so you can access it from any device. Saving your recipes in digital format allows you to keep them safe forever (as long as you back things up or store them someplace like iCloud).

Software like Living Cookbook and Mastercook allow you to create your own recipe book and have many great features that calculate nutritional value, generate shopping lists, allow meal planning and search by ingredient, offer substitution suggestions, import recipes from any source, print your own cookbooks, and adjust recipes for serving amount you select.

There are lots and lots of recipe apps you can find in the iTunes store, which allow you to access an individual cookbook, website, or chef's recipes. Some run a timer to keep you on task to complete the recipe in the indicated time. Others allow you to create a shopping list and are handy to use when you're in the middle of the grocery store and realize you don't know what you need to make that special dinner for your in-laws on Sunday night.

If you'll be using a tablet or smartphone in the kitchen, consider purchasing a holder for it so you can have it upright while you are working. You'll also want to be sure you have a screen protector to guard against spatters.

Capture Family Recipes

Every family has those special recipes that are handed down from generation to generation, or at least special dishes that are made a certain way by your family. You might have grown up loving your grandma's sugar cookies, your dad's barbecue sauce, or your mom's beef stew, but if you don't get the recipe in writing, you'll never be able to replicate it exactly. It's time to pin down those relatives.

The best way to learn exactly how to make a family recipe, if it isn't already written down, is to be in the kitchen when it's being made. Stop and measure everything because a pinch of this and a drop of that mean different things to different people. Write down all the steps involved with details. Consider having a family recipe party, where everybody brings his or her own signature dish and copies of the recipes for everyone else.

If your family has several cooking traditions, consider making a family recipe book. Make a Word document with all the recipes, one per page. Organize them by section. Include fun little tidbits about them, such as how grandma learned to make the recipe, when it was served, and whose favorite it is. Put a family photo on the cover or a photo taken in the kitchen. Take the pages to a copy shop and have them bind it with a spiral binding. You can laminate the cover or pages if you want. This makes an excellent bridal shower or wedding gift for women (or men!) marrying into the family. It's also a thoughtful gift for a young adult who is moving out to his or her first apartment.

To prevent cookbooks from getting dirty and spattered when cooking, invest in a cookbook holder with a protective shield. These products come in various styles and sizes, and they hold your cookbook open to the page you're referring to while protecting the pages. Most are small enough or collapsible for easy storage. Or buy a big beautiful one and regularly change out the cookbook on display.

Food Exploring

There is never any shortage of recipes available if you need ideas. You just have to know where to look. Adding new recipes to your collection keeps you (and your family) interested in cooking and spices things up with new dishes.

Go Online

If you're looking for a recipe for a specific thing, your best bet is to Google it, or go to a big food site like *www.foodnetwork.com* or *www.allrecipes.com*. You'll find many possible versions of the dish you're seeking. Be sure to read the reader reviews to help you determine how tasty, easy, and accurate the recipe is. These sites are also great places to go when you need ideas. Scroll through all the top chicken dishes or type in an ingredient you want to use for ideas.

Read Magazines and Books

Subscribe to cooking and food magazines (such as *Bon Appétit, Taste of Home, Food & Wine, Food Network Magazine,* and *Everyday Food*), or read them at your local library for new recipes. The library is also a great place to browse new (and old cookbooks). Check out the cookbook section of your local bookstore, or surf the cookbook section of an online bookstore for books you might enjoy. There are many online cooking clubs and listservs you can join, where people share recipes or together cook through books as a group.

Ask for the Recipe

When you eat something you enjoy at someone's home, ask for the recipe. Encourage the person to scan and e-mail it to you, which is much less time-consuming than typing it or handwriting it, and gives you more flexibility in how you save it. Take all the new recipes you receive and add them to your recipe collection about once a month, after all your new cooking magazines have come and you've had a chance to look through them. Keep a pile of recipes to be filed with your cookbooks.

Host a Recipe Swap

Plan a recipe swap with friends. Make a date to have a dinner once a month where everyone brings one dish. Bring copies of your recipe to distribute. No one has to cook an entire meal that night!

Trying Out Recipes

It can also be a good idea to temporarily file your new recipes in a special section of your recipe collection called "Recipes to Try," so you can go there when you need an idea and you can also have a chance to try a recipe before you permanently file it in your collection. You could also file the recipe where it belongs and flag it with a sticky note so you can easily find it to try it.

When you add a new recipe to your collection make a note of its source. As you cook with the recipe you may want to add notes on it such as "use less salt" or "add basil." Be sure to write "good" or put a star on recipes that you really like. Over time, you may not remember how much you enjoyed it unless you make a note of it.

Word by Word

If you have a cookbook collection, you know that it can sometimes be hard to fit this into your kitchen. Cabinets are not the ideal way to store cookbooks, and most people need to use their kitchen cabinets for other things if space is at a premium. There are other places to keep your cookbooks so they are accessible.

A bookcase (freestanding or wall mounted) is the ideal location. If you are pressed for space, you'll fit more if you stack them, rather than standing them up.

There are several ways to organize cookbooks. Alphabetically by author's last name or title is one easy way. Most people are looking for something in particular when browsing the cookbook shelves, though, so you may want to try to group them by recipe type (such as baking, general cookbooks, or even categories like cookie, cake, and slow-cooker cookbooks).

Another idea is to group by food ethnicity, which works well if you have several cookbooks featuring foods of different countries. Categories could include Italian, French, Asian, Middle Eastern, Indian, and so on.

If you don't have a bookcase, there are some other areas in the kitchen that can work for cookbook storage. You can stack them on top of the refrigerator or microwave or stand them up with bookends. A basket on the floor can provide cookbook storage space. The top shelf in the pantry is a good spot for cookbooks as well. If you have nowhere else and your collection is small enough, you can place it standing up with bookends on your countertop.

Do not store cookbooks above the stove or oven as the heat and grease can damage them. If you are very short on space, consider breaking up your

EatYourBooks.com is an online index of over 83,000 cookbooks, and 410,000 recipes from them. If you know you saw a great recipe for lemon icebox cake, but can't remember which one of your cookbooks it was in, instead of pulling every book off the shelf, use the site to help locate which book it came from; then find the book and get cooking.

collection. Store three cookbooks next to the dinner plates. Position five in the pantry. Just try to sort them into categories so you know to find the Italian cookbooks next to the pasta and the baking cookbooks in the cupboard with the muffin pan!

Cookbooks are wonderful sources for new recipes, but sometimes it can be hard to keep track of what exactly is in the book that you would like to make. Use small sticky notes to flag pages with things you would like to try. It can also make sense to make a list of the recipes (and page numbers) you are interested in and keep it in the front of the book. You could write the list on one of the blank front pages of the book as well. When you try something in a cookbook and like it, make a note on the page or on a sticky note so you remember how much you enjoyed it.

If you have books which contain just a few recipes you like, photocopy them and put the copies in your recipe collection and donate the book or store it in another room.

Cookbooks can be part of a very attractive display. Try stacking some upright and some on their sides. Intersperse with pottery, antiques, or other items that match your kitchen's theme. You can even use a stack of cookbooks on the floor to create a little table with a plant or basket on top of it.

Culling Your Cookbooks

From time to time, it's a good idea to go through your cookbooks and remove some that you are no longer using. There may be books you received as gifts and don't care for, books that didn't live up to their promise, and books you're tired of. Donate them to your local library for a tax deduction. You may also be able to give them to friends or family members. Consider holding a cookbook swap party where everyone comes with some cookbooks to swap and everyone leaves with some new ones to explore.

Magazine Madness

Cooking magazines can accumulate into big piles very quickly. If you like to keep your cooking magazines after you've read them, organize them into magazine holders. Organize by magazine and by year. If you have room to store these on a shelf in your kitchen, do so, but if not, they can easily be stashed in a closet or even under a bed. Consider buying the yearly index offered by the magazine so you can easily find recipes.

It's fun to keep a few cooking magazines out and about in your kitchen for quick inspiration. The holiday issues in particular often make beautiful accents when left on a table or counter, or in a cookbook holder.

Takeout Time

Let's face it. There are those times when you need to eat, but don't feel like cooking. Takeout to the rescue! Keeping track of all those take-out menus can be a headache. Solve the problem by creating a take-out menu binder. Slide each menu into a plastic sleeve (if it's a foldout menu, get a couple of them and display one page at a time). Keep them in alphabetical order (or use dividers to create ethnic food sections). Keep a little notepad and pen in a pocket in the binder so you can write up your order and have it in front of you when you call it in. You can also create a separate bookmarks section in your Internet browser and keep links to all your favorite menus right there.

Save those plastic take-out food containers! You can reuse them for food storage and they also work well for storing things like cornstarch or cornmeal in the pantry. According to the *Green Guide*, a website and magazine devoted to greener living and owned by the National Geographic Society, the safest plastics for repeated use in storing food are made from high-density polyethylene (HDPE, or plastic #2), low-density polyethylene (LDPE, or plastic #4), and polypropylene (PP, or plastic #5).

Smart Takeout

Takeout is so easy and convenient, but there are some ways to save money and be a little smarter about how you order. If you have extra rice from Chinese or Asian food, freeze it. You'll be able to use it in dishes you cook. Pizza also freezes well, so buy the larger size pizza (which costs less per slice) and freeze the rest for another night. Salads do not keep well (unless you order them with dressing on the side) so don't order more than you need. Sushi will not last and should not be kept more than one day. Don't store your takeout in the cardboard fold-top boxes it comes in. Transfer to plastic or glass storage containers. It will stay fresh longer.

10

COOKING Made Easy

Whether you love cooking or are lukewarm about it, you'll find that being organized about cooking makes your time in the kitchen safer, more productive, less expensive, simpler, and just more fun. Cooking doesn't have to be complicated and messy. It's all in how you approach the task. If you clean up as you go, stay organized, and don't let yourself get overwhelmed, cooking is no different, harder, or messier than any other household task. And in fact, it's lots more fun since you get something yummy when you're done!

Safety First

Food safety is the most important part of any food preparation. It doesn't matter if you prepare gourmet foods that everyone loves; if the food makes people sick, all your work is lost. If you have doubts about the purity or safety of the food, throw it out. These rules apply to all cooking and baking, not just once-a-month cooking.

Foods that could cause trouble if mishandled include all fresh and cured meats (cooked and uncooked), eggs, dairy products like milk and cream, seafood, cooked rice and pasta, opened or unsealed home-canned foods, and all foods that contain any of these ingredients.

Whenever you touch raw meats or uncooked eggs (even the shell!), immediately wash your hands with warm, soapy water before touching anything else. Do not open a cupboard, pick up the salt shaker, or touch anything that will be eaten uncooked. Think about keeping a popup container of hand wipes or a bottle of hand sanitizer in your kitchen for convenience and to help remind you of this important food-safety factor.

More than 75 million cases of food poisoning occur in the United States every year. Almost all could be prevented by cooking food to the proper internal temperature. Follow safe food-handling practices to the letter.

Remember, food poisoning is invisible—it is impossible to tell by taste or smell if food is safe to eat. Most bacteria, and the toxins they produce that cause food-borne illnesses, are not detectable by human senses.

According to the USDA, perishable foods should be left at room temperature for only two hours. After that point, foods must be refrigerated or frozen. Bacteria present in all food grows at temperatures between 40°F and 140°F. Make sure that you keep track of how long potentially hazardous food has been out of refrigeration. Keep raw meats separate from all other foods. Use a separate cutting board, knife, and fork for preparing raw meats.

Even if the bacteria in food are killed in the cooking process, over time, some bacteria produce toxins that are not destroyed by heat or freezing temperatures. Those toxins will make you sick. That's why you must follow food-safety procedures to the letter, heating food quickly, cooling it promptly, and never letting food stand out at room temperature for more than two hours.

If someone in your family falls into a high-risk group (has a compromised immune system or a chronic disease, is elderly, or is under the age of five), you need to be even more careful about food safety. People who fall into these high-risk groups can get so sick from food poisoning they must be hospitalized.

Safe Temps

Meats must be cooked to certain internal temperatures before they are safe to eat. Here are internal temperatures each meat type should reach when it is done:

MEAT COOKING TEMPERATURES	
Type of Meat	Safe Internal Temperature
Chicken parts (light meat)	170°F
Chicken parts (dark meat)	180°F
Whole chickens	180°F
Cuts of beef	145°F
Pork	145°F
Fish	160°F
Ground beef	160°F
Other ground meats	165°F

Check meat with an instant-read meat thermometer. Be sure to wash the thermometer in hot, soapy water in between tests if the meat has not reached the proper temperature the first time you test it.

Get more food safety tips at the USDA website, *www.usda.gov.*

Thawing and Reheating

When thawing meat in the refrigerator, place the bagged or wrapped meat in a container so the juices don't drip on any other food. Never thaw frozen meat at room temperature. You can thaw meat in the microwave oven, but only if you are going to cook it right away.

When you reheat thawed food, be sure it is fully cooked before serving it. Casseroles need to reach an internal temperature of 165°F before they are served. Test the casserole in the very center, since that is the last place to reach proper temperature.

Clean and Safe

Not only is keeping your kitchen clean an absolute must for maintaining an organized environment, it's also critical for maintaining your health. If the kitchen is not kept clean, bacteria and mold can grow on the surfaces and get into your food, which could result in serious illness. Whether you're storing perishable foods, cooking, or cleaning, there are all kinds of safety measures you should take within your kitchen.

The Partnership for Food Safety Education sponsors the Fight Bac! website *www.fightbac.org*, which offers an abundance of information about keeping your food safe from dangerous bacteria. It recommends taking these four primary precautions:

1. **Clean:** Wash hands and surfaces often.
2. **Separate:** Don't cross-contaminate!
3. **Cook:** Cook to proper temperature.
4. **Chill:** Refrigerate promptly.

Putting Food Safety into Practice

When working in the kitchen, wash your hands, utensils, and kitchen surfaces often. After a knife or plate touches raw meat, wash it immediately. Wash your hands, using warm and soapy water, before and after you handle raw foods. Wash your cutting board, dishes, utensils, and countertops after each use (especially after preparing raw meat, poultry, or fish).

Use separate cutting boards for raw meats and vegetables. Store meats, poultry, and fish away from other foods. Wrap or package each type of food separately. See Chapter 7 for information about how long it is safe to refrigerate or freeze certain foods.

Opening the oven door during cooking lets heat out and affects the baking or roasting time of your foods. If you need to look, do so through the oven window. A remote read-out meat thermometer allows you to monitor doneness without letting the heat out.

Basic Cooking Techniques

Even if you are comfortable in the kitchen, you may find this section a handy reminder for decoding recipe instructions. The better you are able to understand recipes, the more organized you will be as you work your way through them.

How to Heat, Cool, Soften, or Melt

Follow these basic rules for heating, cooling, softening, and melting.

- A preheated oven is one that has been turned on and allowed to reach the desired temperature before the food is placed inside. Unless a recipe specifies otherwise, ovens should always be preheated. In most ovens, 10 to 15 minutes is adequate time to preheat.
- Room-temperature foods are those that have been removed from the refrigerator about fifteen minutes before use in a recipe.
- Softened foods are those like butter or cream cheese that have been allowed to stand at room temperature until they are no longer hard to the touch, usually a minimum of 15 minutes.
- Melted foods are foods that have been thoroughly liquefied, either in the microwave or over heat.
- Cooled foods are foods that have been allowed to stand at room temperature for a specified amount of time, or until they can be comfortably touched. Stirring food speeds its cooling time.

- Chilled foods are those that have been allowed to stand in the refrigerator for a specified amount of time, or until both the outside and inside of the food are below room temperature. Stirring food speeds its chilling time.
- *Thoroughly* chilled foods are those that have been allowed to stand in the refrigerator until both the outside and inside of the food have reached the refrigerator's storage temperature. Thorough chilling of heated food usually takes at least an hour or more, depending on the amount of food and shape of the container.
- To soften cold butter or margarine in the microwave: Place 1 stick unwrapped or ½ cup uncovered butter or margarine on a plate. Microwave on low 30 to 45 seconds in a 1,000-watt oven. Adjust time if wattage varies.
- To soften cold cream cheese in the microwave: Place unwrapped cheese on an uncovered plate. Heat on high, 15 to 30 seconds for a 3-ounce package or 30 to 45 seconds for an 8-ounce package. Adjust time if oven wattage is not 1,000.

How to Measure Liquid Ingredients

1. Use a liquid measuring cup—a glass or plastic cup with graduated markings on the side.
2. Place the cup on a flat, level surface.
3. View the liquid at eye level.

Tip: Liquid measuring cups can be greased with a small amount of oil or shortening before measuring thick liquids like honey.

How to Measure Dry Ingredients

1. Use graduated, nesting measuring cups (dry measuring cups).
2. Spoon the ingredient into the appropriate cup, or dip the cup into the container of a dry ingredient.
3. Level it off with a knife or spatula.

Exception: Brown sugar must be packed into the measuring cup, pressing firmly with the fingers. The sugar should retain the shape of the measuring cup when it is dumped.

How to Measure Soft Ingredients

1. Use graduated, dry measuring cups.
2. Fresh breadcrumbs, coconut, shredded cheeses, and similar soft ingredients should be lightly pressed down into the selected measuring cup.

Exception: Solid shortening must be firmly packed down into a dry ingredient measuring cup. Scoop it into the selected cup and pack with a spatula or the back of a spoon, then level off with a spatula or knife.

Slicing, Dicing, and Mixing

It is helpful to familiarize yourself with the different cooking terms for cutting up and mixing food and what these terms mean. You can always refer back to this list if there is any question about a term.

Beat: to stir briskly with a spoon, a whisk, a hand eggbeater, or an electric mixer.

Bias slice: to cut against the grain at an angle.

Blend: to mix two or more ingredients until they make a uniform mixture.

Chop: to cut into small irregular pieces with a knife or food processor.

Core: to remove the center of a fruit like an apple or pear.

Cream: to beat a fat until it is light and fluffy, often in combination with sugar or other ingredients.

Crush: to press or smash seasonings or other foods to release their flavor, using a garlic press, heavy knife, or other implement.

Cube: to cut food into squares about ½" on the sides.

Cut in: to combine a solid fat with dry ingredients, until the fat is in very small pieces about the size of small peas, by using a pastry blender or a fork.

Cut up: to cut into small irregular pieces.

Diagonal slice: to cut at a 45° angle.

Dice: to cut into reasonably uniform pieces of about ¼".

Fold: to combine ingredients gently, using a spatula or spoon to lift ingredients from the bottom of the bowl and "fold" them over the top.

Grate: to rub a food such as cheese, vegetables, or spices against a sharp-edged kitchen tool called a grater, making small or fine particles.

Julienne: to cut into thin strips that look like about 2" long matchsticks.

Knead: to work dough by continuously folding over and pressing down until it is smooth and elastic. Dough can also be kneaded with electric mixer attachments called dough hooks.

Mince: to chop food into very small bits.

Score: to cut through the surface of a food (usually about ¼" deep) to tenderize or make a pattern.

Section: to cut the pulp of a peeled citrus fruit away from the membranes that separate its segments.

Shred: to cut in narrow, thin strips, by using a kitchen shredder or a knife.

Slice: to cut into flat pieces that are usually thin and even.

Snip: to cut herbs or other food into small pieces using kitchen scissors.

Stir: to mix ingredients at a moderate pace to combine them.

Tear: to break into pieces using the hands rather than a knife.

Temper: to gently heat a substance that can curdle (eggs or dairy, usually) before adding to a hot liquid by adding a bit of the hot liquid to the substance and mixing them together. This brings the temperature of the substance closer to the temperature of the hot liquid to prevent curdling.

Toss: to mix ingredients by gently lifting them from the bottom of the bowl and allowing them to tumble, usually using two forks or other utensils.

Whip: to beat rapidly with a wire whisk, hand beater, or electric mixer. Whipping increases volume because it adds air to the ingredient(s).

Food Preparation and Cooking

Basic food preparation and cooking terms you'll need to know:

Bake: to cook food with the indirect dry heat of an oven. Covering food while baking it preserves moistness; leaving food uncovered results in a drier or crisp surface.

Barbecue: to cook with barbecue sauce or spices, or to cook slowly on a grill or spit, usually outdoors.

Baste: to spoon or pour broth, sauce, or other liquid over food while cooking to prevent dryness or add flavor.

Blacken: to cook Cajun-seasoned foods over a very high heat.

Blanch: to cook fruits, vegetables, or nuts very briefly in boiling water or steam, usually to preserve the color or nutritional value or to remove the skin. This process is also called parboiling.

Boil: to cook a liquid at a temperature at which bubbles rise and break on the surface. To bring to a boil means to heat just until bubbling begins. In a full or rolling boil, the bubbles are larger and form quickly and continuously.

Braise: to cook food slowly in a tightly covered pan in a small amount of liquid. Usually, food is first browned in a small amount of fat. Braising tenderizes food and can be done either on the stovetop or in the oven.

Bread: to coat foods before cooking in breadcrumbs or cracker crumbs.

Broil: to cook food directly under a direct source of intense heat or flame, producing a browned or crisp exterior and a less well-done interior.

Caramelize: to coat the top of a food with sugar and then broil it quickly until the sugar is melted. Or, to melt sugar in a saucepan over a low heat until it turns into a golden syrup. Caramelizing can also mean melting the sugar in a certain food (onions or beef, for example) to give it a brown color and bring out its slightly sweet flavor.

Deep-fry: to cook food in hot, liquefied fat (usually kept at 350° to 375°F) that is deep enough to cover and surround the food completely.

Deglaze: to add liquid to a skillet in which meat has been cooked, stirring to loosen meat bits and make a broth. The broth can be used to make a sauce.

Dot: to place pieces of butter randomly on top of a food.

Drizzle: to pour a liquid topping in thin, irregular lines over a food.

Dust: to sprinkle a dry ingredient lightly and fairly evenly over a food.

Fry: to cook in hot fat or oil, producing a crisp exterior.

Glaze: to spread a thin coating such as jelly on food, making it appear glossy.

Grease: to coat the surface of a pan with shortening or cooking spray to prevent foods from sticking while they bake. To "grease and flour" is to dust the pan lightly with flour after applying the shortening.

Grill: to cook foods directly above a source of intense heat or flame. Foods can be pan-grilled on a stovetop by using a specially designed pan with raised grill ridges.

Marinate: to let food stand in a special liquid to flavor it or tenderize it. The liquid is called a marinade.

Oven-fry: to cook food, usually breaded, in a hot oven with a small amount of fat, usually dotted or drizzled on top of the food.

Pan-fry: to fry with little or no added fat, using only the fat that accumulates during cooking.

Parboil: see Blanch.

Poach: to cook in a simmering (not boiling) liquid.

Purée: to make into a thick liquid, usually by using a blender or food processor.

Reduce: to boil a liquid until some of it evaporates, thus concentrating the flavor.

Roast: to cook meat or poultry in the indirect heat of the oven, uncovered. Roasted foods are not cooked in added liquid (compare Braise), but are often basted with liquids for flavor and moistness.

Sauté: to cook in a small amount of fat over high heat.

Scald: to heat a liquid to just below the boiling point, when small bubbles begin to appear around the edges of the pan. When milk is scalded, a film will form on the surface.

Sear: to brown on all sides over high heat to preserve juiciness.

Sift: to process dry ingredients through a kitchen sifter or sieve. Sifting adds air to dry ingredients that have been compressed in storage and also removes any lumps.

Simmer: to keep a liquid just below the boiling point; a few bubbles will rise and break on the surface.

Skim: to remove fat or foam that has accumulated on the surface of a liquid, usually using a spoon.

Steam: to cook food above (not in) boiling or simmering water.

Stew: to cook food, covered, very slowly in liquid.

Stir-fry: to cook small pieces of food in a hot wok or skillet, using a small amount of fat and a constant stirring motion.

Basic Cooking Tips

Keep these tips and hints in mind while cooking to make things easy, safe, and fun.

- Always wash hands before preparing food.
- Always use pot holders to take a pan from the oven. To indicate that a pan is hot from the oven, carefully mark it with flour or a pot holder on the edge of the pan.
- Keep handles of pots and pans on the stove turned in from the edge.
- Prevent steam burns by opening pot lids away from you.
- Never leave knives in the sink. Knives should be hand-washed after each use.
- Always use a timer when baking.
- Use an oven thermometer for accurate oven temperature.
- Use a meat thermometer to check internal temperature of foods.
- Keep a fire extinguisher close by for emergencies.
- Never throw water on a grease fire. Smother it with a pot lid if possible.
- Wipe up spills on the floor right away. Sprinkle salt or flour on the floor where there has been a greasy spill to absorb the oil before wiping up.

Swapping It Out

To make cooking easier, post these lists of measurement conversions and recipe substitutions inside one of your cabinet doors for quick reference:

MEASUREMENT CONVERSIONS	
½ teaspoon =	30 drops
1 teaspoon =	⅓ tablespoon *or* 60 drops
3 teaspoons =	1 tablespoon *or* ½ fluid ounce

MEASUREMENT CONVERSIONS

½ tablespoon	=	1½ teaspoons
1 tablespoon	=	3 teaspoons *or* ½ fluid ounce
2 tablespoons	=	⅛ cup *or* 1 fluid ounce
3 tablespoons	=	1½ fluid ounces *or* 1 jigger
4 tablespoons	=	¼ cup *or* 2 fluid ounces
5⅓ tablespoons	=	⅓ cup *or* 5 tablespoons + 1 teaspoon
8 tablespoons	=	½ cup *or* 4 fluid ounces
10⅔ tablespoons	=	⅔ cup *or* 10 tablespoons + 2 teaspoons
12 tablespoons	=	¾ cup *or* 6 fluid ounces
16 tablespoons	=	1 cup *or* 8 fluid ounces *or* ½ pint
⅛ cup	=	2 tablespoons *or* 1 fluid ounce
¼ cup	=	4 tablespoons or 2 fluid ounces
⅓ cup	=	5 tablespoons + 1 teaspoon
⅜ cup	=	¼ cup + 2 tablespoons
½ cup	=	8 tablespoons or 4 fluid ounces
⅝ cup	=	½ cup + 2 tablespoons
⅔ cup	=	10 tablespoons + 2 teaspoons
¾ cup	=	12 tablespoons *or* 6 fluid ounces
1 cup	=	16 tablespoons *or* ½ pint or 8 fluid ounces
2 cups	=	1 pint *or* 16 fluid ounces
1 pint	=	2 cups *or* 16 fluid ounces
1 quart	=	2 pints *or* 4 cups *or* 32 fluid ounces
1 gallon	=	4 quarts *or* 8 pints *or* 16 cups *or* 128 fluid ounces

COMMON INGREDIENT SUBSTITUTIONS

Ingredient	Amount	Substitution
Allspice	1 teaspoon	½ teaspoon cinnamon, ¼ teaspoon ginger, and ¼ teaspoon cloves
Baking powder	1 teaspoon	¼ teaspoon baking soda plus ½ teaspoon cream of tartar *or* ¼ teaspoon baking soda plus ½ cup buttermilk (decrease liquid in recipe by ½ cup)
Beer	1 cup	1 cup nonalcoholic beer *or* 1 cup chicken broth
Brandy	¼ cup	1 teaspoon imitation brandy extract plus enough water to make ¼ cup
Bread crumbs	1 cup	1 cup cracker crumbs *or* 1 cup matzo meal *or* 1 cup ground oats
Broth: beef or chicken	1 cup	1 bouillon cube plus 1 cup boiling water *or* 1 tablespoon soy sauce plus enough water to make 1 cup *or* 1 cup vegetable broth
Brown sugar	1 cup, packed	1 cup white sugar plus ¼ cup molasses and decrease the liquid in recipe by ¼ cup *or* 1 cup white sugar *or* 1¼ cups confectioners' sugar
Butter (salted)	1 cup	1 cup margarine *or* 1 cup shortening plus ½ teaspoon salt *or* ⅞ cup vegetable oil plus ½ teaspoon salt *or* ⅞ cup lard plus ½ teaspoon salt
Butter (unsalted)	1 cup	1 cup shortening *or* ⅞ cup vegetable oil *or* ⅞ cup lard
Buttermilk	1 cup	1 cup yogurt *or* 1 tablespoon lemon juice or vinegar plus enough milk to make 1 cup
Chocolate (semisweet)	1 ounce	1 (1-ounce) square of unsweetened chocolate plus 4 teaspoons sugar *or* 1 ounce semisweet chocolate chips plus 1 teaspoon shortening
Chocolate (unsweetened)	1 ounce	3 tablespoons unsweetened cocoa plus 1 tablespoon shortening or vegetable oil
Cocoa	¼ cup	1 (1-ounce) square unsweetened chocolate

COMMON INGREDIENT SUBSTITUTIONS

Ingredient	Amount	Substitution
Corn syrup	1 cup	1¼ cups white sugar plus ⅓ cup water *or* 1 cup honey *or* 1 cup light treacle syrup
Cottage cheese	1 cup	1 cup farmer's cheese *or* 1 cup ricotta cheese
Cream (half and half)	1 cup	⅞ cup milk plus 1 tablespoon butter
Cream (heavy)	1 cup	1 cup evaporated milk *or* ¾ cup milk plus ⅓ cup butter
Cream (light)	1 cup	1 cup evaporated milk *or* ¾ cup milk plus 3 tablespoons butter
Cream (whipped)	1 cup	1 cup frozen whipped topping, thawed
Cream cheese	1 cup	1 cup puréed cottage cheese *or* 1 cup plain yogurt, strained overnight in a cheesecloth
Cream of tartar	1 teaspoon	2 teaspoons lemon juice or vinegar
Crème fraîche	1 cup	Combine 1 cup of heavy cream and 1 tablespoon of plain yogurt. Let stand for 6 hours at room temperature.
Egg	1 whole (3 tablespoons or 1.7 ounces)	2½ tablespoons of powdered egg substitute plus 2½ tablespoons water *or* ¼ cup liquid egg substitute *or* ¼ cup silken tofu puréed *or* 3 tablespoons mayonnaise *or* half a banana mashed with ½ teaspoon baking powder *or* 1 tablespoon powdered flaxseed soaked in 3 tablespoons water
Evaporated milk	1 cup	1 cup light cream
Fats for baking	1 cup	1 cup applesauce *or* 1 cup fruit purée
Flour—bread	1 cup	1 cup all-purpose flour plus 1 teaspoon wheat gluten (available at health-food stores and some supermarkets)
Flour—cake	1 cup	1 cup all-purpose flour minus 2 tablespoons
Flour—self-rising	1 cup	⅞ cup all-purpose flour plus 1½ teaspoons baking powder and ½ teaspoon of salt

COMMON INGREDIENT SUBSTITUTIONS

Ingredient	Amount	Substitution
Garlic	1 clove	⅛ teaspoon garlic powder *or* ½ teaspoon granulated garlic *or* ½ teaspoon garlic salt—reduce salt in recipe
Ginger—dried	1 teaspoon	2 teaspoons chopped fresh ginger
Ginger—fresh	1 teaspoon, minced	½ teaspoon ground, dried ginger
Green onion	½ cup chopped	½ cup chopped onion, *or* ½ cup chopped leek *or* ½ cup chopped shallots
Herbs—fresh	1 tablespoon chopped fresh	1 teaspoon (chopped or whole leaf) dried herbs
Honey	1 cup	1¼ cups white sugar plus ⅓ cup water *or* 1 cup corn syrup *or* 1 cup light treacle syrup
Hot pepper sauce	1 teaspoon	¾ teaspoon cayenne pepper plus 1 teaspoon vinegar
Ketchup	1 cup	1 cup tomato sauce plus 1 teaspoon vinegar plus 1 tablespoon sugar
Lard	1 cup	1 cup shortening *or* ⅞ cup vegetable oil *or* 1 cup butter
Lemongrass	2 fresh stalks	1 tablespoon lemon zest
Lemon juice	1 teaspoon	½ teaspoon vinegar *or* 1 teaspoon white wine *or* 1 teaspoon lime juice
Lemon zest	1 teaspoon	½ teaspoon lemon extract *or* 2 tablespoons lemon juice
Lime juice	1 teaspoon	1 teaspoon vinegar *or* 1 teaspoon white wine *or* 1 teaspoon lemon juice
Mace	1 teaspoon	1 teaspoon nutmeg
Margarine	1 cup	1 cup shortening plus ½ teaspoon salt *or* 1 cup butter *or* ⅞ cup vegetable oil plus ½ teaspoon salt *or* ⅞ cup lard plus ½ teaspoon salt

COMMON INGREDIENT SUBSTITUTIONS

Ingredient	Amount	Substitution
Mayonnaise	1 cup	1 cup sour cream *or* 1 cup plain yogurt
Milk—whole	1 cup	1 cup soy milk *or* 1 cup rice milk *or* 1 cup water or juice *or* ¼ cup dry milk powder plus 1 cup water *or* ½ cup evaporated milk plus ½ cup water
Molasses	1 cup	Mix ¾ cup brown sugar and 1 teaspoon cream of tartar
Mustard—prepared	1 tablespoon	Mix together 1 tablespoon dried mustard, 1 teaspoon water, 1 teaspoon vinegar, and 1 teaspoon sugar
Onion	1 cup, chopped	1 cup chopped green onions *or* 1 cup chopped shallots *or* 1 cup chopped leeks *or* ¼ cup dried minced onion *or* ¼ cup onion powder
Orange zest	1 tablespoon	½ teaspoon orange extract *or* 1 teaspoon lemon juice
Parmesan cheese	½ cup, grated	½ cup grated Asiago cheese *or* ½ cup grated Romano cheese
Pepperoni	1 ounce	1 ounce salami
Pumpkin pie spice	1 teaspoon	½ teaspoon cinnamon *plus* ¼ teaspoon ground ginger plus ⅛ teaspoon ground allspice plus ⅛ teaspoon ground nutmeg
Raisins	1 cup	1 cup dried currants *or* 1 cup dried cranberries *or* 1 cup chopped, pitted prunes
Ricotta	1 cup	1 cup dry cottage cheese *or* 1 cup silken tofu
Rum	1 tablespoon	½ teaspoon rum extract, plus enough water to make 1 tablespoon
Saffron	¼ teaspoon	¼ teaspoon turmeric
Semisweet chocolate chips	1 cup	1 cup chocolate candies *or* 1 cup peanut butter or other flavored chips *or* 1 cup chopped nuts *or* 1 cup chopped dried fruit

COMMON INGREDIENT SUBSTITUTIONS

Ingredient	Amount	Substitution
Shallots, chopped	½ cup	½ cup chopped onion, *or* ½ cup chopped leek *or* ½ cup chopped green onion
Shortening	1 cup	1 cup butter *or* 1 cup margarine minus ½ teaspoon salt from recipe
Sour cream	1 cup	1 cup plain yogurt *or* 1 tablespoon lemon juice or vinegar plus enough cream to make 1 cup *or* ¾ cup buttermilk mixed with ⅓ cup butter
Sour milk	1 cup	1 tablespoon vinegar or lemon juice mixed with enough milk to make 1 cup: Let stand 5 minutes to thicken.
Soy sauce	½ cup	4 tablespoons Worcestershire sauce mixed with 1 tablespoon water
Stock—beef or chicken	1 cup	1 cube beef or chicken bouillon dissolved in 1 cup water
Sweetened condensed milk	1 (14-ounce) can	¾ cup white sugar mixed with ½ cup water and 1⅛ cups dry powdered milk: bring to a boil and cook, stirring frequently, until thickened, about 20 minutes
Vegetable oil— for baking	1 cup	1 cup applesauce *or* 1 cup fruit purée
Vinegar	1 teaspoon	1 teaspoon lemon or lime juice *or* 2 teaspoons white wine
White sugar	1 cup	1 cup brown sugar *or* 1¼ cups confectioners' sugar *or* ¾ cup honey *or* ¾ cup corn syrup
Wine	1 cup	1 cup chicken or beef broth *or* 1 cup fruit juice mixed with 2 teaspoons vinegar *or* 1 cup water
Yeast—active dry	1 (.25-ounce) package	1 cake compressed yeast *or* 2½ teaspoons active dry yeast *or* 2½ teaspoons rapid rise yeast
Yogurt	1 cup	1 cup sour cream *or* 1 cup buttermilk *or* 1 cup sour milk

Organized Cooking

Your time in the kitchen can be streamlined and made more efficient so that you can get more done in the same amount of time. It's always best to start working in a clean kitchen. You have more room to work and everything you might need will be clean.

- Before you begin preparing a meal, think about what you're making and what you will need to cook it. Getting your pots, utensils, and foods out makes it much easier to cook without having to run around pulling things out of the pantry and cupboards.
- Make sure you read recipes through completely before you begin cooking, so you don't realize too late you were only supposed to add half of the sugar at the beginning of the recipe, or that your eggs are supposed to be at room temperature.

Ready at the Same Time

One thing people worry about when cooking meals is getting all the food ready at the same time. It's nearly impossible to have everything ready at the same second; instead, you need to think about what foods can sit or be reheated and let those get done first. Things like fish, soufflé, or turkey cutlets that you want to serve right at the moment they are done should be the things you wait for. So if you're making sautéed sole, you've got to have your potatoes and vegetables ready the moment the fish is. The potatoes can sit in a warm oven and the vegetables can be cooked, drained, and returned to their pots with lids on to sit a few minutes. If they need reheating, add a little butter and turn the burner back on for just a minute or two.

Heavy, thick meats like whole chickens, roasts, and whole tenderloins hold their heat for quite a while, so if they're done before the sides, that's okay. Keep in mind that most whole meats should be allowed to rest for at least five minutes before you serve them; this buys you time to get your other dishes done.

Always set the timer for baked goods or anything else that is supposed to cook for a set time period. You might think you'll remember to take it out in fifteen minutes, but then the phone will ring or your kids will need something and you'll forget.

Shortcuts

We all need some time savers to make life in the kitchen easier. These tips will help you streamline your efforts in the kitchen.

- Cook large batches and store. If you're making rice, cook a large batch and freeze it. If you're browning ground beef, brown a lot of it. Use the rest in recipes later in the week or freeze it for future use. Poach or grill enough chicken breasts to make several meals or dishes (use extra in sandwiches and salads). Always double or triple your recipes if you are making something that can be frozen. It takes almost no additional time and it gets meals in the freezer for those desperation dinners. If you're chopping onions, consider if you will need them for other recipes later in the week. If so, chop enough at once. When making cookies, double the batch and freeze the additional amount. Make it into a log and wrap it in plastic wrap. You'll be able to slice and bake when you take it out of the freezer.
- Instead of using a double boiler, melt chocolate in the microwave. Cook for only thirty seconds at a time, stirring in between and take it out before it is completely melted. It will melt as it stands.
- When you cook pasta, always bring your water to a boil; then add the pasta. Salting the water will help it boil faster and a teaspoon of olive oil will keep the pasta pieces from sticking to each other.
- Wash your produce when you bring it home from the store, before you put it away. This way everything in the fridge is completely table and recipe ready.
- Instead of sifting dry ingredients, use a wire whisk to stir them in a bowl.
- Bake two things at once in your oven to save energy and to save on preheating time. Covered pots and pans cook more quickly, so always put a lid on it.
- If you need to slice meat very thinly, pop it in the freezer until it begins to harden and you'll easily be able to slice it.

- Peel vegetables over a paper towel or piece of newspaper, then just throw the whole thing out.
- Put a bowl on the counter that will be your garbage bowl while cooking.
- Place a rubber band over a corner of a cutting board to keep it from slipping.
- Place a damp towel under a mixing bowl to keep it in place.
- Get your hands wet before forming meatloaf or meatballs. The food won't stick to your hands.
- Season your steaks as you are wrapping them for the freezer. They'll be ready to go right on the grill when you take them out.
- Use a small funnel to separate an egg. The yolk will get caught and the whites will run out.
- Smash your garlic cloves with the side of a knife and the skins will easily come off.
- To easily peel a tomato, drop it in boiling water for about twenty seconds. The skin will come right off.
- Use an ice cream scoop to fill your muffin tins with batter. It's exactly the right amount.
- Line baking sheets with parchment paper for no cleanup.
- Set the table when you unpack the dishwasher. There's no reason to put it all in the cupboards and take it all out again later.
- Roll a lemon on the counter with your hands before juicing it. The juice will come out more easily and you'll get more.
- Always crack eggs into small bowls before adding them to recipes. This way it is easy to get out any shell that falls in.
- Refrigerate an onion or run it under cold water before peeling and chopping it to reduce onion tears.
- Add a splash of white vinegar to the water when you hard-boil eggs to make the shells easy to peel off.
- Shred cold butter with a cheese grater before using it in a baking recipe. You can avoid trying to soften it in the microwave.
- Put a marshmallow at the bottom of an ice cream cone. It will absorb the melted ice cream and prevent messy leaks.
- Microwave potatoes for three minutes before using them in a dish. They will cook much faster.

Making a List and Checking It Twice

"There's nothing to eat!" It's always a challenge to help kids learn to find (healthy) food on their own, whether they're putting together their own breakfasts, packing lunches, looking for snacks, or making dinner for themselves on an "every man for himself" kind of night. To make things easier, create a list of foods you have in the house for each category and post it on the fridge, inside the pantry, or inside a cabinet door.

So, under "breakfast," you could list bagels, oatmeal, hard-boiled eggs, cold cereal, etc. Under dinner items, cooked brown rice, cold chicken legs, bag of salad, and sliced melon. Update the list weekly so your kids always have suggestions about what to eat.

Frugal Fun

If you are organized when you cook, you can find many ways to use things twice, extend the life or usefulness of some ingredients, and get the most use out of things. It takes a little organization though to save these items you normally would throw away.

- The freezer is your friend. Designate a space in the freezer for your reusable items. Freeze soft or spotted bananas in the skin and use to make banana bread later. Freeze lemon rinds and use for zest in future recipes. Keep your marshmallows in the freezer to prevent them from getting old. When you buy bacon, separate it out into portions and wrap each portion in plastic wrap and freeze. You won't waste any. Save stale bread in a bag in the freezer and use it for breadcrumbs or stuffing. Use teabags twice, keeping them in a bag in the freezer in between uses. Save the rinds from cheeses in the freezer and toss them into soups for additional flavor. Toss leftover veggies from dinner into a container in the freezer. The next time you make soup or stew, dump them in.
- Keep the parts you don't use. If a recipe calls for an egg yolk, save the egg white to use in an omelet or in other recipes. If you use half an onion in one recipe, put the rest in a zip-top bag in your vegetable drawer and

use at another time. Designate an area in your fridge for these tidbits so you will always know where to look for items you can repurpose.

- Use the leftovers. For example, keep the bones from a roasted chicken and make your own stock. Put it in a stockpot and add water (covering the carcass), a carrot, stalk of celery, bay leaf, and half an onion, along with salt and pepper. Boil then simmer on low for several hours until the joints fall apart. Strain. Use leftover roast chicken to make chicken salad. Use leftover fruit to make fruit salad. Always label leftovers so you know how old they really are (see Chapter 12 for more information).
- Use everything down to the last bit. For example, use butter wrappers to grease pans instead of expensive cooking spray. Store them in a zip-top bag in your butter compartment.
- When you think all the dish soap is used up, add a little water to the bottle and swish it. You'll get several more uses.
- Buy big and break things down; for example, buy whole heads of lettuce instead of bags of salad. Separate out into meal-size portions in zip-top bags and it will be ready to grab for dinner. Buy blocks of cheese and shred them yourself instead of buying bags of shredded cheese. Chop leftover garlic and put it in a little jar with olive oil to cover it. Use in future recipes.

Shake It Up

An organized kitchen allows you to feel more relaxed and more able to have fun while cooking. And the more fun you can have while cooking, the more likely you are to do it. If it's not a chore (and it won't be, once you've done a full organization), the time will go quickly and you'll feel more positive about your outcomes. There's much to love about cooking—the smells, the time away from work or the computer, the delicious tastes, making something for your family, and being able to say, "I made that!"

Get Organized

First things first. Get your kitchen (and yourself) organized so that you have a routine in the kitchen that relaxes you. Put on some music. Almost everyone cooks better to good tunes. The music helps you relax and gets you in the groove. If you're not in the mood for music, but have a TV in the kitchen, put on a cooking show. Cooking with someone else is fun, even if they're on TV.

Invite Your Family to Join In

And speaking of cooking with someone else, get your family and friends into the action. Cook a meal together with each person responsible for a dish, or work on a big project like making cookies together. Talk, laugh, tell stories, sing, dance, and tell jokes. The kitchen is about bonding and laughter.

Experiment

Even if you think you can't really cook without a recipe, you definitely can. Make a salad and try it with different veggies, cheeses, or toppings. Bake a potato and choose toppings to go on that. Toss some veggies into the next pasta dish you make, even if your sauce comes from a jar. Listen to your individual tastes and desires and let them guide you. Feeling adventurous? Make up your own marinade for some chicken breasts or build on a soup recipe to answer your cravings.

Accept the Mess

Don't get upset about the mess. A little soap and water and it will all disappear. Cleanup is part of the fun. You wash and I'll dry. Make it a team effort.

Lots of people find cooking a stressful activity. As with anything else in life, the more you do it, the easier it gets. One big pressure is that you're trying to feed people and if the food doesn't turn out, what will you do? Be organized enough so that you practice all recipes on your immediate family before you try them on others. If they flop, you can have the backup plan to order a pizza or make peanut butter and jelly sandwiches and laugh about it. If you're cooking for guests, always plan to make enough of the other items so that if one thing on the menu does not turn out, there will still be enough food to go around. Remember, it's just cooking, not an exam.

11

Foolproof RECIPES

Whether you are a fantastic cook or someone who doesn't feel very confident about cooking, it's important to have a stable of basic recipes on which you rely and to which you can turn. This chapter offers solid recipes for many categories of food, so you can have a fallback for every situation in which you might need a recipe. Knowing you have a recipe that will work will help you feel more confident and organized as you go about life in your kitchen.

TORTILLA PINWHEELS

Serves 8

These festive hors d'oeuvres are also called Mexican Sushi because of their ingredients and their appearance. They resemble the California Rolls you may get at a sushi bar but they taste like a deluxe taco treat! This is an easy recipe to have in your collection.

2 bunches green onions
16 ounces cream cheese, softened
8 ounces sour cream
¼ cup salsa
¼ cup black olives, chopped
½ teaspoon garlic powder
8 ounces Cheddar cheese, grated
¼ bunch fresh cilantro, chopped
10 large (burrito size) flour tortillas

1. Set aside 10 whole green onions. Chop the remaining green onions (green and white parts) and put into a mixing bowl.
2. Add cream cheese, sour cream, salsa, olives, garlic powder, Cheddar cheese, and cilantro to the chopped green onions and mix together thoroughly.
3. Lay a tortilla flat and spread 4 tablespoons of the cream cheese mixture over it. Put a whole green onion on the edge of the tortilla and roll tortilla into a log, squeezing firmly as you roll. Repeat with remaining tortillas, green onions, and filling.
4. Wrap each log in plastic wrap and refrigerate for 4 hours.
5. Unwrap plastic and cut each log into 1-inch-thick slices. Arrange on a platter, and serve.

ARTICHOKE DIP

Serves 4

Perfect for any party, this baked dip can be served hot from the oven accompanied by crusty French bread slices. It will look like you spent a lot more time on it than you did.

2 15-ounce cans artichoke hearts, drained and rinsed
1 red bell pepper, chopped finely
1 green bell pepper, chopped finely
3 cloves garlic, minced
2 cups mayonnaise
White pepper
1 pound Parmesan cheese, grated

1. Preheat the oven to 325°F.
2. Mix together all ingredients except ¼ of the Parmesan cheese and place into a 9" × 9" baking dish or 1½-quart casserole dish.
3. Sprinkle the remaining Parmesan cheese over the top of mixed ingredients and bake for 45 minutes or until golden brown. Serve with crackers or bread.

MINESTRONE

Serves 6

This Italian classic is filling and warm. Serve it with some warm Italian bread and some grated Parmesan cheese to sprinkle on top. It makes a full meal.

½ cup chopped onion

½ cup chopped carrots

¼ cup chopped celery

2 tablespoons olive oil

2 cloves garlic, minced

¼ cup chopped spinach

1 cup chopped cabbage

32 ounces chicken broth

2 cups chopped zucchini

1 cup chopped, peeled tomatoes

½ cup cut green beans

½ cup broken spaghetti

Salt and pepper to taste

1. Sauté the onions, carrots, and celery in the olive oil over medium heat for 15 minutes.
2. Add garlic, spinach, and cabbage, and cook until greens are wilted.
3. Add chicken broth, zucchini, tomatoes, and green beans. Bring to a boil.
4. Simmer for 15 minutes. Add the spaghetti and simmer 15 minutes more.
5. Season soup with salt and pepper.

CHICKEN SOUP

Serves 8

This is the traditional cure for the common cold! Buy chicken already cut into parts or cut up a whole chicken yourself. If you're in a hurry, make this with chopped rotisserie chicken and cook only until the vegetables are soft. Add cooked noodles or cooked rice before serving if you like.

4 cups water
4 cups chicken broth
1 4-pound chicken, cut in 8 pieces
4 carrots, peeled and sliced into ½" pieces
1 large onion, diced
2 stalks celery, sliced into ½" pieces
1 clove garlic, sliced
3 peppercorns
1 bay leaf
½ teaspoon turmeric
Salt to taste
Chopped fresh parsley
1 recipe Matzo Balls (see this chapter), if desired

1. Put the water, chicken broth, chicken, vegetables, peppercorns, and bay leaf in a large soup pot. Bring to a boil and simmer uncovered for 2 hours.
2. Using a slotted spoon, remove the chicken from the broth and set aside until it is cool enough to handle.
3. Remove bay leaf and peppercorns from soup broth and add turmeric and salt to taste.
4. Remove the bones and skin from the chicken meat and discard. Chop the meat into bite-sized pieces and return it to the soup broth.
5. Serve soup sprinkled with parsley.

SOUPS & SALADS

SOUPS & SALADS

MATZO BALLS

Serves 8–10

4 eggs

2 tablespoons olive oil

2 tablespoons water

2 teaspoons salt

2 teaspoons chopped dill

1 cup matzo meal

1. Using a fork, mix eggs and olive oil in a bowl.
2. Add water, salt, and chopped dill; mix.
3. Add cup matzo meal; mix.
4. Cover; refrigerate 15 minutes.
5. Scoop walnut-size balls with wet fingers and drop into boiling water or broth.
6. Cook for 35 minutes. Serve in chicken soup.

COBB SALAD

Serves 6

This is a California-born classic. It is a hearty salad that includes a variety of ingredients for a depth of flavor and texture. The Cobb Salad was invented at the Brown Derby restaurant in Los Angeles, a famous hangout of stars and gossip columnists since its opening in 1926.

1 head iceberg lettuce, chopped
½ cup vinaigrette or bottled Italian dressing
2 diced tomatoes
½ cup diced cooked chicken
1 diced avocado
½ cup crumbled blue cheese
¼ cup bacon bits (bottled or freshly fried and crumbled bacon)
3 hard-boiled eggs, chopped
½ cup whole chopped green onions
1 recipe Vinaigrette Dressing (below)

1. Toss lettuce leaves with dressing. Mound dressed lettuce on an oval platter.
2. Top dressed lettuce with all the other ingredients arranged in separate strips.

VINAIGRETTE DRESSING

Serves 6

½ cup olive oil
2 tablespoons red wine or cider vinegar
2 teaspoons Dijon mustard
1 teaspoon sugar
½ teaspoon Italian herb mix
¼ teaspoon garlic powder
½ teaspoon Worcestershire sauce
Salt and pepper to taste

Place ingredients in a bottle or plastic container and shake.

FRENCH TOAST

Serves 4

French toast, known in France as pain perdue ("lost bread"), is delicious served with warm maple syrup and powdered sugar. Use white bread, challah, French bread, sourdough, or brioche for variety. For a do-ahead dish, you can also place the bread in a baking pan, cover with the other ingredients and let it soak overnight; then bake in a 350°F oven for 30 minutes.

6 eggs
1½ cups milk
1 teaspoon vanilla extract
½ teaspoon cinnamon
8 tablespoons butter
8 slices day-old bread
¼ cup powdered sugar

1. Using a whisk, combine eggs, milk, vanilla, and cinnamon in a shallow, flat bowl (like a soup or pasta bowl). Melt butter in a frying pan over medium heat, being careful not to let it burn.
2. Dip both sides of each slice of bread in the custard mixture and immediately pan-fry in melted butter on both sides.
3. Cut French toast in triangular halves and sprinkle with powdered sugar.
4. Serve with butter and warm maple syrup.

VARIATION: CROISSANT FRENCH TOAST
To make croissant French toast, use 1 croissant per person. Freeze croissant to make slicing easier. Using a serrated bread knife, slice croissant horizontally into 3 slices. Dip in regular French toast custard (egg and milk mixture—above) to which 1 teaspoon orange zest has been added. Fry in butter in a nonstick pan. Serve with fresh strawberries and powdered sugar.

BLUEBERRY MUFFINS

Serves 12

This basic muffin recipe can be used to make different muffins by substituting blackberries, raspberries, cranberries, chocolate chips, peaches, or pecans for the blueberries. Add orange zest to the cranberry, lemon zest to the blueberry, or chopped hazelnuts to the chocolate chip for more variety.

2 cups all-purpose flour
⅔ cup sugar
1 tablespoon baking powder
½ teaspoon salt
2 eggs
1 cup milk
6 tablespoons butter, melted
1 teaspoon vanilla extract
1½ cups fresh or frozen blueberries

1. Preheat oven to 400°F. Grease a 12-cup muffin tin or line it with fluted paper cups.
2. Combine flour, sugar, baking powder, and salt in a large bowl using a whisk.
3. Combine eggs, milk, butter, and vanilla in another bowl using a whisk.
4. Stir the wet ingredients into the dry ingredients; then fold in blueberries with a spatula. Fill muffin cups with the batter, distributing the batter evenly.
5. Sprinkle tops with sugar. Bake 15 minutes.

QUICHE

Serves 6

Quiche, a savory egg tart, is a custard with cheese and various add-ins baked in a pastry shell. The classic Quiche Lorraine has sautéed onions and bacon, but no cheese. Broccoli, ham, roasted red bell peppers, and sautéed mushrooms make good quiche add-ins. The cheese can be any kind you like. This works for dinner, lunch, or brunch.

½ recipe Pie Dough Crust (recipe in this chapter), prebaked in 9" tart pan with removable bottom; or a store-bought pie crust, prebaked

½ cup diced leeks, white part only

1 tablespoon olive oil

1 cup shredded smoked Gouda cheese

¼ cup baby spinach leaves, packed into measuring cup

2 tablespoons julienned, sun-dried tomatoes

3 eggs

1½ cups heavy cream

$\frac{1}{16}$ teaspoon nutmeg

½ teaspoon salt

3 drops cayenne pepper sauce

¼ teaspoon white pepper

2 tablespoons chopped fresh chives

1. Preheat oven to 375°F.
2. Sauté leeks in olive oil until tender. Spread them on the bottom of the pre-baked pastry shell. Sprinkle cheese on top of leeks. Tuck spinach leaves here and there in the cheese. Distribute the tomatoes evenly on top.
3. Combine eggs, cream, nutmeg, salt, cayenne pepper sauce, and white pepper. Stir in chives.
4. Pour egg mixture over the ingredients in the tart shell, gently pressing down on anything that floats to the top so that everything stays submerged.
5. Bake for 30 minutes, until set. Serve warm. If you like, you also can chill, slice, and reheat the quiche in an oven or toaster oven.

TUNA NOODLE CASSEROLE

Serves 6

This recipe is the real thing from scratch and is perfect for potlucks, or to freeze. It is just as easy as a packaged mix, and you get to control the seasonings and quality of ingredients. This recipe uses crushed potato chips for a topping, but you can use breadcrumbs instead for a more elegant presentation. Enrich the recipe with 1 cup shredded Cheddar cheese stirred in before baking.

8 ounces egg noodles, cooked

1 cup sliced mushrooms

2 tablespoons butter

2 tablespoons all-purpose flour

2 cups milk

2 cans tuna, drained

¾ cup frozen peas

Salt and pepper to taste

1 cup crushed potato chips

1. Preheat oven to 375°F and butter a 9" × 13" casserole dish. Lay cooked noodles in the dish.
2. Sauté mushrooms in butter, sprinkle with flour, and cook for a few minutes. Add milk, and cook until thickened. Stir in tuna and peas. Season with salt and pepper.
3. Pour mushroom sauce mixture over noodles and gently toss if necessary to distribute evenly.
4. Sprinkle potato chips over the top and bake for 20 minutes.

CASSEROLES

REAL MACARONI AND CHEESE

Serves 6

This is a kids' classic that is not just for kids! This recipe can be divided into individual portions and frozen before it is baked, and then baked at a later date for a quick weeknight dinner. Substitute whole-grain pasta for a bigger nutritional kick.

4 tablespoons butter

¼ cup all-purpose flour

1 teaspoon dry mustard

2¾ cups milk

1 teaspoon salt

⅛ teaspoon pepper

Pinch cayenne pepper

3 cups shredded Cheddar cheese

16 ounces elbow macaroni, cooked and drained

1 cup dry breadcrumbs

1. Preheat oven to 350°F. Butter a 9" × 13" baking dish.
2. Melt the butter in a medium-size saucepan. Stir in the flour and dry mustard; cook, stirring constantly, over medium heat for 2 minutes.
3. Add the milk and whisk over medium heat until mixture thickens, whisking constantly to prevent burning on the bottom. Stir in the salt, pepper, and cayenne pepper. Remove from heat.
4. Stir in the cheese and let the mixture sit for a minute. Stir again to smooth out the melted cheese.
5. Pour cooked macaroni into the casserole dish; add cheese sauce. Mix until macaroni is coated with cheese.
6. Sprinkle breadcrumbs on top of the casserole and bake for 45 minutes, until browned and bubbly on the edges. Serve warm.

LASAGNA

Serves 12

Lasagna is the perfect one-pot dinner. It also freezes well and is a wonderful item to bring to people who need meals brought in. Add a box of defrosted spinach that's been drained to this for some extra color and fiber.

5 cups tomato sauce

1 pound ground beef, browned and drained

1-pound box lasagna noodles

3 eggs

16 ounces ricotta cheese

2 cups shredded mozzarella cheese

½ cup chopped fresh parsley

½ cup grated Parmesan cheese

Salt and pepper to taste

1. Preheat oven to 350°F. Oil a lasagna (baking) pan and spread 1 cup tomato sauce on the bottom. Mix the remaining tomato sauce with the cooked ground beef. Set aside.
2. Cook the lasagna noodles in boiling water. (Be sure to take them out before they are completely done—about 1 minute before package instructions suggest—so they don't overcook when you bake the lasagna.) Place one layer of noodles over the sauce layer in the pan.
3. In a bowl combine the eggs, ricotta, and 1 cup mozzarella cheese until well blended. Stir in the parsley and salt and pepper to taste.
4. Spread half of the ricotta mixture over the noodles in the pan. Top the ricotta with a layer of noodles. Ladle 2 cups of the meat sauce over the noodles; top with another layer of noodles.
5. Spread the remaining ricotta mixture over the noodles. Top with the last of the noodles. Ladle the remaining meat sauce over the noodles.
6. Scatter the remaining mozzarella cheese over the sauce; sprinkle with the Parmesan cheese. Bake for 1 hour and 25 minutes.

PASTA

POT ROAST

Serves 4

What tastes better on a cold night? An Italian variation for this meal, which adds tomatoes, garlic, and wine, can be found following the recipe. This recipe is a basic meat-and-potatoes version that can be expanded on with whatever flavor elements you like. Use the leftover meat for sandwiches, or turn the meat and vegetables into potpie.

> 1 large onion
> 1- to 2-pound beef roast
> 3 carrots, peeled
> 2 celery stalks
> 2 large potatoes, peeled
> 1 cup beef broth
> ½ teaspoon salt
> ¼ teaspoon pepper
> 1 tablespoon chopped parsley

1. Preheat oven to 325°F.
2. Cut onion into large chunks and scatter them on the bottom of a roasting pan.
3. Put the meat on top of the onions.
4. Cut the carrots, celery, and potatoes into 2" chunks and scatter them around the meat. Pour the broth over the meat. Sprinkle the salt, pepper, and parsley over the meat and vegetables.
5. Cover and roast in the oven for 2–2½ hours.

VARIATION: ITALIAN POT ROAST

Make your pot roast with tomato juice and red wine instead of beef broth and add canned diced tomatoes, oregano, and basil. Poke holes in the meat with a paring knife and insert garlic slices before cooking. Serve sliced pot roast and vegetables over creamy polenta.

MEATLOAF

Serves 4

Meatloaf can be cooked with a variety of toppings, such as ketchup, barbecue sauce, brown sugar, mustard, onions, or beef broth. Leftovers make great sandwiches.

⅔ pound ground beef

⅓ pound ground pork

¼ cup shredded carrots

¼ cup minced onion

½ teaspoon celery salt

1 tablespoon Dijon mustard

1 tablespoon ketchup

1 teaspoon Worcestershire sauce

1 egg

1 tablespoon chopped fresh parsley

Salt and pepper

¼ cup oatmeal

¼ cup breadcrumbs

3 slices bacon

1. Preheat oven to 350°F.
2. In a bowl, using your hands, combine all ingredients except for the bacon.
3. Shape into a loaf and press into a loaf pan.
4. Line the top of the meatloaf with bacon slices.
5. Bake until meat thermometer inserted in the center of the meatloaf reads 160°F, which should be after about 1¼ hours.

ENTRÉES

ENTRÉES

OVEN-ROASTED WHOLE CHICKEN

Serves 4

It doesn't get more classic than this, and it also doesn't get much easier! This entrée works for everyday, or for company. Use leftovers to make chicken salad or sandwiches.

1 4-pound roasting chicken, rinsed, giblet pack removed
Salt and pepper
1 bay leaf
1 onion, quartered
1 tablespoon paprika
1 teaspoon herbes de Provence or dried thyme
1 teaspoon each salt and pepper

1. Preheat oven to 400°F. Season inside of bird with salt and pepper, then put bay leaf and onion inside. Tuck wings under the back of the bird.
2. Mix together paprika, herbs, 1 teaspoon each salt and pepper, and rub the mixture all over the chicken's skin. Place chicken in a roasting pan, breast-side up.
3. Roast the chicken uncovered in the oven until you can move the legs easily and juices run clear, about 1½ hours.

SOLE AMANDINE

Serves 6

Sole cooks quickly, so have everything else ready to go when you put this in the pan. It looks like it took a lot more work than it really does!

> 1½ pounds sole fillets
> ½ cup Wondra flour
> ¼ cup butter
> ½ cup sliced almonds
> 2 tablespoons grated lemon rind
> Salt and pepper to taste
> 2 tablespoons lemon juice

1. Dust the fish with the flour, shaking off excess.
2. Place half the butter in a large, nonstick frying pan and melt over medium-high heat.
3. Place the fish in the pan; cook for three minutes, then flip.
4. Continue to cook until fish is completely opaque, depending on thickness, about 2–4 minutes.
5. Remove fish from the pan and place remaining butter, almonds, lemon rind, salt and pepper, paprika, and lemon juice in the pan. Stir until almonds begin to brown. Pour sauce and almonds over fish.

RICE PILAF

Serves 4

Rice pilaf goes with almost anything, so it's a great recipe to keep handy. Substitute brown rice for white rice in this for more whole-grain goodness.

8 tablespoons unsalted butter

½ cup diced onion

1 cup long-grain rice

12 ounces low-sodium chicken broth

½ teaspoon salt

¼ teaspoon white pepper

1 bay leaf

1. Preheat oven to 350°F.
2. In a saucepan over medium heat, melt butter. Sauté the onion in butter until tender.
3. Add rice; sauté for 3–5 minutes with the onion.
4. Pour rice mixture into a 9" × 13" baking dish. Add chicken broth, salt, pepper, and bay leaf. Stir to incorporate.
5. Cover and bake for 45 minutes. Remove bay leaf before serving.

CREAMED SPINACH

Serves 4

Creamed spinach is a delicious classic. Use skim milk to cut down on calories in this dish.

¼ cup diced onion
2 tablespoons butter
2 tablespoons all-purpose flour
1 cup milk
Pinch of nutmeg
1 teaspoon salt
¼ teaspoon pepper
4 cups cooked spinach leaves, chopped
2 tablespoons grated Parmesan cheese

1. Sauté onion in butter until translucent.
2. Sprinkle onion with flour and cook over medium heat for a few minutes.
3. Stir in milk; cook, stirring frequently, until mixture starts to thicken.
4. Season the sauce mixture with nutmeg, salt, and pepper.
5. Stir in the spinach and cheese; heat through.

SIDE DISHES

SCALLOPED POTATOES

Serves 4

Add 2 ounces chopped ham to this to make it an entrée.

4 large russet potatoes, peeled

¼ cup all-purpose flour

1 teaspoon salt

½ teaspoon pepper

1 cup milk

¼ cup butter, melted

¼ cup grated Parmesan cheese

1. Preheat oven to 350°F. Butter a 9" × 13" baking dish; set aside.
2. Slice the potatoes into ¼-inch-thick slices.
3. Put down a layer of ⅓ of the potato slices in the baking dish and sprinkle half of the flour over them. Then sprinkle ⅓ of the salt and pepper over this layer.
4. Add another layer of potatoes, the rest of the flour, and ⅓ of the salt and pepper on top of the first layer. Top this layer with a final layer of potatoes and the final ⅓ of the salt and pepper.
5. Pour milk over the potatoes; then drizzle the melted butter and sprinkle the cheese over the top. Cover and bake for 1 hour, until potatoes are tender and can be pierced easily with the tip of a paring knife.

OVEN-ROASTED RED POTATOES

Serves 4

Crunchy and tasty, yet so simple to make, these potatoes are an excellent accompaniment to any dinner. They're particularly yummy when served with fish or chicken.

3 pounds small red potatoes
2 tablespoons olive oil
1 teaspoon salt
½ teaspoon pepper
½ teaspoon dried thyme

1. Preheat the oven to 350°F.
2. Cut the potatoes in quarters. In a large bowl, toss potatoes with oil and seasonings.
3. Spread the potatoes out on a sheet pan and roast uncovered for 45 minutes.

STEAMED ASPARAGUS WITH HOLLANDAISE SAUCE

Serves 4

The hollandaise sauce can be used in many other ways, such as a sauce for beef tenderloin or over grilled salmon.

> 1 bunch asparagus, trimmed
> Hollandaise Sauce

1. Steam the asparagus for 5–10 minutes until tender.
2. Serve with hollandaise sauce.

HOLLANDAISE SAUCE

> 2 egg yolks
> ½ tablespoon cold water
> 4 tablespoons melted butter
> ½ teaspoon lemon juice
> Pinch cayenne pepper
> Salt and white pepper to taste

1. Whisk egg yolks and water in a stainless-steel or glass bowl over simmering water (making sure that the bowl is a bit larger than the pot containing the simmering water) and cook until mixture thickens to ribbon stage. (The ribbon stage is the point in cooking a liquid mixture when, if a whisk is dipped into the liquid and raised a few inches above the pot, the liquid forms a "ribbon.")
2. Slowly pour melted butter into yolks, drop by drop at first, whisking constantly. Continue whisking, pouring the butter in a thin stream, after the sauce starts to thicken.
3. Remove bowl from heat and whisk in the lemon juice and cayenne pepper.
4. Season sauce with salt and white pepper to taste.

BISCUITS

Serves 8

This biscuit dough can be cut into smaller rounds to make mini biscuits, too. Serve the warm biscuits with butter, honey, jam, sausage patties, or ham for breakfast, or serve them with dinner instead of dinner rolls.

3 cups all-purpose flour
4½ teaspoons baking powder
1½ teaspoons salt
1 tablespoon sugar
6 tablespoons cold butter
1¼ cups buttermilk

1. Preheat oven to 400°F.
2. Combine flour, baking powder, salt, and sugar in a mixing bowl.
3. Cut butter into small pieces and add to dry ingredients. Mix butter into dry ingredients with a pastry cutter or with your fingers. This mixture should be a bit lumpy so biscuits turn out flaky.
4. Add buttermilk and mix with a wooden spoon to form the dough.
5. Roll dough on a floured board to 1-inch thickness. Cut dough into circles with a 2–3-inch round cookie cutter or a drinking glass. Place rounds on an ungreased baking sheet and bake 12 minutes.

APPLE PIE

Serves 8

Apple pie is always a winner, and you can make it at all times of the year since apples are always available. This delicious two-crusted pie is suitable for any occasion. A combination of Granny Smith and Golden Delicious apples provides a nice texture and sweet-tart flavor.

Pie Dough Crust, 2 rolled-out circles (recipe in this chapter)
5 cups peeled, cored, apples, cut into ¼" slices
4 tablespoons cornstarch
½ cup sugar
1 tablespoon cinnamon
4 tablespoons butter, cut in pieces
2 tablespoons sugar, for sprinkling on top crust

1. Preheat oven to 350°F.
2. Line pie pan with one of the pie dough circles.
3. Mix apples in a bowl with cornstarch, sugar, and cinnamon.
4. Pile the apples into the dough-lined pie pan, and then dot them with the butter. Cover apples with the remaining pie dough circle. Crimp edges together to seal the crust. Cut four 1" slits around the center of the pie to allow steam to escape during baking.
5. Brush the crust with water and sprinkle with sugar. Bake for 1 hour.

PIE DOUGH

This flaky pie dough recipe will make enough dough for 2 single-crust 9" pies or one double-crust 9" pie. If you can't find pastry flour, all-purpose flour may be substituted. Rolled-out dough circles can be made in advance and frozen or refrigerated until you are ready to use them.

2¼ cups pastry flour
4½ teaspoons sugar
¾ teaspoon salt
1½ cups cold unsalted butter
½ cup ice water

1. Combine flour, sugar, and salt in a bowl.
2. Cut butter into ½" slices.
3. Mix butter into dry ingredients with a pastry cutter or a knife and fork until butter is in pea-sized lumps.
4. Add ice water (ice cubes removed) to flour/butter mixture, stirring with a wooden spoon to combine and form the dough.
5. Divide dough in half and form into two balls. Wrap in plastic and refrigerate for 1 hour before rolling into 10" circles.

NOTE: PREBAKE (ALSO CALLED BLIND-BAKE)

To blind-bake a pie crust (bake it without browning), line a pie pan with pie dough, put coffee filters over the dough, and fill the filters with dried beans or pie weights. Bake at 350°F until set, about 25 minutes. Remove beans and coffee filters and bake crust about 10 minutes more, until crust is a light golden brown in color.

CHOCOLATE CHIP COOKIES

Yields 2 dozen

These cookies can also be made with chocolate chunks instead of chips. Other variations include adding white chocolate chips or 1 cup of chopped nuts. This dough can be rolled into a log, wrapped in plastic, and refrigerated or frozen for future use.

2 cups unsalted butter, softened
1 cup dark brown sugar
1 cup sugar
2 eggs
1 teaspoon vanilla extract
2 cups all-purpose flour
1 teaspoon salt
1 teaspoon baking soda
1 cup semisweet chocolate chips

1. Preheat oven to 350°F.
2. With an electric mixer, cream together the butter, brown sugar, and sugar until fluffy.
3. Add eggs and vanilla; combine well. Scrape down the sides of the bowl.
4. Mix the flour, salt, and baking soda together in a bowl. Add the flour mixture to the butter mixture, mixing by hand with a wooden spoon to combine into a smooth dough. Stir in chocolate chips.
5. Using two spoons, drop dough in mounds onto an ungreased cookie sheet. Bake cookies 12 minutes. Cool on a rack.

BROWNIES

Yields 16

This recipe uses both cocoa and chocolate chips to create a double chocolate brownie. You may add a variety of things to this batter before baking, such as chopped nuts, chopped candy bars, or dried fruits. The brownies can be sprinkled with powdered sugar or covered in chocolate frosting (recipe in this chapter) after they have cooled.

> 12 tablespoons unsalted butter, melted
> 1½ cups sugar
> 2 eggs
> ½ teaspoon vanilla extract
> 2 tablespoons water
> ¾ cup unsweetened cocoa powder
> ½ cup all-purpose flour
> ½ teaspoon salt
> ½ teaspoon baking powder
> 1 cup semisweet chocolate chips

1. Preheat oven to 350°F. Grease a 9" × 13" baking dish.
2. Mix together the butter and sugar in a mixing bowl.
3. Beat the eggs into the butter mixture; then stir in the vanilla and water.
4. In a separate bowl, combine the cocoa powder, flour, salt, and baking powder. Add this dry mixture to the wet mixture; stir to combine. Stir in the chocolate chips. Scrape the batter into the prepared baking dish, and smooth out the top of the batter.
5. Bake brownies for 30 minutes. Cool slightly in pan, and then cut into 16 squares. Serve warm or at room temperature.

CHOCOLATE CAKE

Serves 12

This chocolate cake is a classic three-layer cake that can be served with a glass of milk, whipped cream, or ice cream. If you don't want to make a fancy layer cake you can bake this cake in a 9" × 13" baking dish, frost it, and cut into squares.

16 tablespoons unsalted butter, softened

2½ cups sugar

4 eggs

1 teaspoon vanilla extract

2¾ cups all-purpose flour

2 teaspoons baking soda

½ teaspoon baking powder

½ teaspoon salt

2 cups hot water

1 cup cocoa powder

Chocolate Frosting (recipe in this chapter)

1. Preheat oven to 350°F. Butter and flour three 9" round cake pans.
2. Combine hot water and cocoa powder; set aside to let cool.
3. In a large bowl, beat butter, sugar, eggs, and vanilla together for 5 minutes with an electric mixer.
4. In another bowl combine the flour, baking soda, baking powder, and salt. Add dry ingredients to the butter mixture in thirds, alternating with the cocoa mixture. Scrape down the sides of the bowl to make sure everything is well incorporated.
5. Divide batter evenly among the prepared cake pans. Bake for 20–25 minutes, until a toothpick inserted in the center comes out clean. Set pans on rack for 10 minutes; then turn layers out onto racks. If the layers stick in the pan, try carefully running a butter knife around the perimeter of the pan to loosen cake from the side of the pan.
6. When completely cool, frost tops of two cake layers with Chocolate Frosting; stack them; put third layer on top. Spread frosting on the top and sides of the layer cake.

CHOCOLATE FROSTING

Serves 12

16 ounces semisweet chocolate chips
2 ounces unsweetened baking chocolate
7 ounces water
1¼ cups unsalted butter

1. Chop chocolates into small chunks and put them into a metal or glass bowl. Add water.
2. Set the bowl over simmering water. Stir occasionally to combine chocolate with the water as it melts.
3. Cut butter into chunks and stir it into the chocolate mixture.
4. When chocolate and butter have melted, remove the bowl from the simmering water and whisk the frosting to combine. It will be melted and liquid at this point. Set the bowl in a cool place (not the refrigerator) to set.
5. Stir the frosting occasionally while it is cooling to achieve a smooth, creamy consistency. This will take at least 6 hours. Before frosting a cake, whisk the frosting to fluff it up a bit.

DESSERTS

CHEESECAKE

Serves 12

This recipe is for a basic creamy cheesecake that can be served plain or with a variety of toppings and sauces, such as jam swirled on top before baking.

½ cup all-purpose flour

2 tablespoons sugar

6 tablespoons butter, melted

½ cup ground almonds

24 ounces cream cheese (do not use whipped cream cheese), softened

2 cups sugar

2 tablespoons cornstarch

3 eggs

3½ cups sour cream

1 teaspoon vanilla extract

1. Preheat oven to 350°F. In a bowl combine flour, 2 tablespoons sugar, melted butter, and ground almonds with a rubber spatula. Press mixture into the bottom of a springform pan that has been sprayed with cooking spray. Bake for 10 minutes. Remove from oven and set aside.
2. With an electric mixer, beat the cream cheese until fluffy. Add 1½ cups of the sugar and the cornstarch; cream together. Beat in eggs one at a time, scraping down the sides of the bowl after each one. Stir in 1½ cups of the sour cream.
3. Pour this batter into the springform pan and bake for about 1 hour. The middle of the cheesecake should jiggle slightly when finished. Remove from oven and cool at room temperature. Refrigerate and chill completely overnight.
4. With an electric mixer, whip the remaining 2 cups of sour cream with the remaining ½ cup sugar and the vanilla.
5. Top the chilled cheesecake with the whipped sour cream mixture; smooth the top. Let the cake set in the refrigerator, covered, for 1–2 hours before serving.

12

MEAL PLANNING
Made Easy

There's more to meal planning than opening the fridge and hoping to find something you can get on the table before your stomach (or your family) riots. With a little thought, planning, and perhaps some advance prep, you can make meals something that happen with little angst, and no takeout unless you really want it! You can plan meals to make a week or a month ahead. You can cook and freeze meals for your family in a madcap assembly line once a month, and you can plan for leftovers. However you go about it, a little bit of planning will make your time in the kitchen feel organized and calm.

Healthy Habits

Recent research indicates that many serious diseases such as heart disease, certain cancers, diabetes, and high blood pressure are diet-related. The typical American diet contains far more fat than is healthy, and surprisingly, about twice as much protein as is necessary. The USDA provides dietary guidelines that will help you plan healthy meals.

Dietary Guidelines

The most important part of planning meals for yourself and your family is to make sure the meals are healthy. Half of the plate in front of each person should be made up of fruits and vegetables. At least half of the grains your family eats should be whole grains. Proteins should be lean proteins, like chicken with the skin and visible fat removed. The USDA shares its food plate (the replacement for the food pyramid) at *www.choosemyplate.gov*, where you can see what portion sizes should look like and get tips for nutrition for all of your family members.

Check the Label

Nutrition labels also show the percentage of recommended daily nutrient intake contained in a serving of food. These percentages are based on the United States Department of Agriculture Food and Nutrition Service estimate of 2,000 calories per day for the average daily diet. Actual caloric intake will and should vary with age, gender, weight, and activity level. In general, men and young adults need more calories than do women and older adults. Pregnant and breastfeeding women need more calories, as well.

Based on 2,000 calories per day, the USDA suggests the following nutrient levels:

RECOMMENDED DAILY AMOUNTS OF NUTRIENTS	
Nutrient	Amount
Total fat	Less than 65 grams
Saturated fat	Less than 20 grams
Cholesterol	Less than 300 milligrams
Sodium	Less than 2,400 milligrams
Total carbohydrate	300 grams
Dietary fiber	25 grams

The USDA also recommends:

- Maintaining a diet high in grains, vegetables, and fruits.
- Maintaining a diet low in fat, saturated fat, and cholesterol.
- Maintaining a diet with a moderate intake of sugar and salt.
- Eating a variety of foods.

Proteins Are Key

Proteins are the "building blocks" of the body. They are necessary for the growth, maintenance, and rebuilding of every cell. The most concentrated sources of protein are animal products. Animal proteins, which include meat, fish, eggs, and milk, contain all of the nine essential amino acids that proteins can provide and are called complete proteins. Vegetable proteins are present in nuts, seeds, whole grains, and legumes. All vegetable proteins, however—with the one exception of soy—are incomplete. If animal sources of protein are not included in the diet, vegetable proteins must be combined carefully to supply the body with all essential amino acids. This is why many vegetarians take supplements to achieve a well-balanced diet.

Carbohydrates for Energy

Carbohydrates provide most of the body's energy. Simple carbohydrates include all kinds of sugars and are sweet. Complex carbohydrates include grain products and some fruits and vegetables, such as beans and potatoes. Because complex carbohydrates must be split apart during the digestive process before they can be absorbed by the body, they supply energy over a longer period of time than do simple carbohydrates. Complex carbohydrates also contain vitamins, minerals, and dietary fiber. Fiber is the part of a plant that cannot be digested by humans. Water-insoluble fiber, found in fruits, vegetables, and grains, stimulates and regulates the digestive tract. Water-soluble fiber, present in fruits, vegetables, oat bran, and beans, may slow the absorption of sugar into the bloodstream and reduce blood cholesterol levels.

Fat Isn't Always Flab

Although they have a deservedly bad name, fats are necessary to good health in appropriate amounts. They provide body insulation, cushioning, and energy reserve, and allow the body to use fat-soluble vitamins. In addition, fats make the body feel full or satisfied after eating.

Cholesterol is not a fat, but is a substance that is present in some fats. It is necessary for proper functioning of nerves and hormones. The human liver can manufacture all the cholesterol the body needs. However, dietary cholesterol is also present in some foods. A high level of cholesterol in the blood is related to cardiovascular disease.

Saturated Fats

Fats contain both saturated- and unsaturated-essential fatty acids. Saturated fats not only contain dietary cholesterol but also encourage the body to produce more than it needs. All animal fat is saturated fat. Two plant fats—palm and coconut oils—are also heavily saturated. Both are used extensively in processed- and packaged-bakery products, sweets, snacks, and other junk foods.

Unsaturated fats, which include most vegetable fats, are actually believed to reduce blood cholesterol levels when they replace saturated fat in the diet. Monounsaturated fats include fish oils and olive, canola, and peanut oils.

Polyunsaturated fats are found in tuna and salmon, and in sunflower, corn, and sesame oils. However, partially hydrogenated vegetable oils (although unsaturated) contain trans-fatty acids, which research indicates may raise blood cholesterol. Partially hydrogenated oils are used in many shortenings and margarines.

Fat Figures

The American Heart Association recommends a diet in which not more than 30 percent of total caloric intake is from fats. The nutrition labels that now appear on most cans, milk cartons, and other food packages show how much protein, carbohydrate, and fat a serving contains in gram weight. A calorie measures the energy value of food, not its fat content.

Charted Territory

The best way to stay organized and plan your meals is to create a meal chart. Plan out what you will cook for every dinner and write it down. You can do this a week or a month in advance. Some meal planners make up a list of two months' worth of meals, and then just rotate them throughout the year.

If you're planning for the next week, make a list and stick it inside a cupboard door or on your fridge for easy consultation. Check out the list when making your shopping list for that week. If you want to plan for a month, print out a calendar page for that month and write the meals on that.

You definitely want to plan an entrée for each night. If you are planning weekly, it makes sense to plan your sides as well. If you're planning monthly, chart your entrées for the month; then plan sides out as you come to each week, before you do the grocery shopping for that week.

Think Seasonally

When making up a meal chart, take the seasons into consideration. You'll want to include dishes that take advantage of fresh local produce that is available at that time. People's tastes and cravings also change with the seasons. In the summer, you may not want to cook a casserole that is hot and heavy and instead might feel happier with some grilled fish or a cold chicken salad.

The opposite is true in cold weather. Make your plan so that you can grill in the warmer months and use your oven more in the winter months.

To Each His Own

When planning out what meals you'll be making, think about your family's likes and dislikes. There's no sense in including dishes most people in your family won't eat and you'll want to be sure that family favorites are strongly represented in your plan. Also, don't forget to be nutritionally minded, and plan meals that are balanced.

Spontaneity

While it's tempting to fill in a chart for a week or a month with a planned meal each night, there are going to be nights when all you really want is a take-out pizza or when you just have to try a new recipe you ripped out of a magazine. Leave a few nights per month blank to allow you to move things around to accommodate these kinds of spur-of-the-moment desires.

Rotate

Make sure you rotate your meals well. Don't plan beef two nights in a row or have the same dish twice in one week. You also don't want to have the same menu every Monday. Planned menus should not feel boring or too routine.

Designate Jobs

When you plan out a whole week's worth of meals, or a whole month's worth, you can think about who is going to do all the work. When it's just you scrambling to throw some dinner together, there isn't much opportunity to enlist help, other than having someone else set the table. When you plan your meals, plan the work as well. Set up a schedule alternating children to do the dishes each night. Create a plan whereby a high school child can put a casserole in the oven and make a salad one night a week. Delegate carrot peeling to someone else in the house. Think about who can do what and write it right on your meal schedule.

Benefits of Planning

Doing all this planning might seem like a lot of work. It does take some time and consideration, but it has many benefits. You can sit down and do all the planning at once. Get out your cookbooks, your coupons, and your list of freezer and pantry items (see Chapters 6 and 7) to maximize your savings and incorporate all the dishes you want to make. Grocery shopping becomes a snap. No more wandering through the aisles looking for inspiration and trying to figure out what you can buy that you can cook for the next few days. You'll know exactly what you'll need when you get to the store. You can buy things in bulk or in large quantities on sale because you have a plan for how you will use them.

Knowing the plan will help you save time because you'll be able to do some prep work that will work for several recipes. It's also, frankly, a big stress reliever. Scurrying to get some dinner on the table each night can really add to your stress. Knowing exactly what you'll be making, and that you have all the ingredients on hand makes your life so much easier.

You won't be tempted to buy fast food. You and your family will sit at the table and eat together. You'll know exactly what your family is eating and will be sure it meets current dietary guidelines. You'll spend time together and have the chance for face-to-face conversations.

Mark Your Territory

How many times have you planned a meal, bought everything you need, then gone to make it only to discover someone in your house ate an ingredient before you could use it? Once you know what items you plan to use in cooking in the next week, mark them so no one eats them! Place a piece of masking tape on the item or a colored sticker which will tell everyone in your house "hands off!" You may also want to set aside a section in your pantry to stash ingredients for meals you have planned and let everyone know it's off limits.

Monthly Meal Cooking

Another way to plan your menus is to do monthly cooking. Once-a-month cooking is a marathon cooking session that involves deciding what you want to cook for a whole month of meals, making lists, shopping, and then preparing and freezing enough meals to last for a whole month—all on one day or over a weekend. With organization, planning skills, and some food-science knowledge, you will never need to order takeout again. You'll pull delicious, healthy meals out of your freezer and reheat them in minutes. Simple recipes freeze best. Avoid recipes with complicated sauces, different cooking times, multiple preparation steps, and those that use exotic ingredients.

Mix and Match

Think about serving one recipe in different ways. For instance, a beef chili recipe can be served over taco chips and garnished with salsa, cheese, and lettuce as a taco salad. The same recipe can be served over baked potatoes or as a topping for hot dogs. This planning allows you to vary the meals you serve using your tried-and-true recipes, combining similar preparation and cooking steps.

When you are compiling your list of recipes, think not only about the foods your family likes, but also about what's on sale that week at your local supermarket. For instance, if your grocer has a special on ground beef in five-pound packs, pull recipes for meatloaf, spaghetti sauce, and beef manicotti from your collection.

Variety Is Key

As with menu planning, make sure to cook a good variety of recipes for the month. For instance, choose several chicken casseroles, two grilled beef recipes, three slow cooker recipes, one chicken and one ham sandwich recipe, and a pepperoni pizza. Write down the recipes you have chosen on a blank calendar page; it's easier to make sure that you are serving your family a good variety of flavors, textures, colors, and nutrients during the month when you can see the whole month's plan at a glance.

Cooking Day Dos

Since you're going to be spending an entire day cooking, the most important "do" of all is to enjoy the process. Enjoy the sounds of cooking: the knife blade *chunking* into the chopping board, foods *sizzling* in a pan, and even the *clinking* of metal on metal as you flip through nested measuring spoons. Think about all the time you're going to save, and how well you are treating yourself and your family. In addition:

- Do stock up on paper towels and dishrags.
- Do make sure you have several large plastic garbage bags available, and remove each bag from the kitchen as soon as it is full.
- Do cook with a helper or two. Split up some of the chores; for instance, one person can cook a few recipes while the other keeps the kitchen clean, and then switch places.
- Do keep a first-aid kit handy. When you're working with this much food and so many appliances, it pays to be prepared.
- Do make sure your knives are sharp and in good condition. A sharp knife slices more easily and is actually safer to use than a dull knife. Dull knives can slip as you work with them, making it all too easy to cut yourself.
- Do make an inventory before you start, to make sure you have enough pots, pans, spoons, forks, and knives on hand, and that they are all in good working order.
- Do make sure that all your appliances are in good working order and are accurate.
- Do schedule more time than you think you'll need.
- Do take breaks where you leave the kitchen, sit down, and sip some tea while putting your feet up. Nobody can work for seven or eight hours without a break.
- Do think about prepping some of the food on the same day that you shop. You could cut up some vegetables or meats and package them in plastic containers, or start meat cooking in your slow cooker for the next day.

And a Few Don'ts

The most important "don't" of all: don't wear yourself out or undertake a day of cooking if you don't feel well. If you're unsure of your strength or stamina, start small by choosing just a few meals to make and freeze. Here are some other important don'ts:

- Don't attempt too much, especially on your first experience with this type of cooking. It's much easier to schedule another cooking session if you aren't exhausted by the first attempt.
- Don't shop and do all your cooking on the same day.
- Don't let prepared food sit on the counter while you assemble other recipes. As soon as the recipes are prepared, cool them; then pack, label, and freeze them.
- Don't cook a meal for your family or yourself on monthly cooking day. Go out to eat! You deserve some pampering after your marathon-cooking session.

Try to make your cooking session fun. If you see it as a positive challenge and do everything you can to make the process enjoyable, you are going to want to schedule another session.

Cook with a partner—a neighbor, relative, or work colleague. Think about organizing a cooking club and pair off with a different member each month. Your recipe collection will expand exponentially, and you'll pass along this efficient and money-saving cooking method to more people. You will not only expand your collection of freezable recipes, but the time will go by much more quickly when another person is there to share the chores.

Enjoy the aromas as your home fills with delicious smells. Who needs potpourri or air fresheners when bread, cookies, casseroles, and vegetables are baking and simmering? And enjoy the safe, cozy feeling of "putting food by" to feed your family and friends.

Recipes for a Month

While you can certainly plan to cook thirty individual recipes for freezing, it's much easier to cook double or triple amounts of ten to fifteen recipes. You'll save lots of time and energy by doubling or tripling a recipe and packaging and freezing that food in meal-size portions. Then rotate the food into your meal plan for the month.

It's important to make sure the recipes you have chosen are cooked with different methods. For instance, you don't want to have thirty baked dishes unless you have three or four ovens. Choose some recipes that are cooked in a skillet or saucepan, some that are baked, some that are frozen without cooking, some that are grilled, and some that are prepared in a slow cooker.

When choosing your recipes, you can make adjustments to streamline cooking. For instance, if one recipe calls for ground beef with onions and garlic and another uses just ground beef and onions, add garlic to the second dish or omit garlic from the first one so you can prepare the foods together.

Make notes as you go through preparation and cooking, to improve your assembly-line process, refine shopping lists and organization of tools and ingredients, and streamline recipe preparation.

Shortcuts

Consider using some of these quick options to keep shopping and cooking easy and organized:

- Buy prepared vegetables from a salad bar in your supermarket.
- Purchase cooked rice from a local Chinese restaurant.
- Buy coleslaw mix instead of shredding cabbage; purchase one head of cabbage for the recipe that requires whole leaves.
- Purchase twice as much meatloaf mix instead of some each of ground beef and ground pork.

Remember, these shortcuts will cost more than buying items that aren't "value added." Decide whether your budget can handle these added conveniences, and whether the time you will save is worth the extra cost.

Planning and Preparation

There are some tasks that you can do ahead of cooking day. Place all nonperishable foods on your kitchen table in groups as they are needed for the recipes to make sure you have all the ingredients on hand. This can be done two to three days ahead of cooking day. You can precook chicken, brown beef, peel and chop onions and garlic, seed and chop peppers, chop vegetables, make pie crust, and cook rice and pasta.

Label foods accurately as you go along. Once meals are wrapped and frozen, it will be difficult to identify them. Waterproof markers, grease pencils, and wax markers work well on most freezer wrap and plastic containers. Be sure to record the name of the recipe, the date it was prepared, thawing and reheating instructions, and additional foods needed to finish the recipe.

Lovely Leftovers

Leftovers get a bad rap. They don't have to be the dregs of meals past that no one wants to eat. Leftovers can be some of the most in-demand items in your kitchen if you approach them with the right attitude and a little planning. After all, Paula Deen says "Bein' rich is havin' leftovers."

Leftovers can save your life! If you know you have a busy week, make twice as much of a dish you know your family likes and stash the rest in the fridge for a desperation dinner later in the week. Cook once, eat twice. The great thing is leftovers require only the ability to push a button (on the microwave) which just about anyone in your family can do, so you can use leftovers for nights you're too tired or too busy cook, or even not home at all.

Leftovers can be used in other ways as well. Think about how you can use food you're cooking in lunches, those that are packed or eaten at home. Leftover salads, pastas, and soups are great for at-home lunches. Cooked chicken, turkey, and ham are perfect for packed sandwiches. If your kids make their own sandwiches, slice the meat before refrigerating it. Make sure everyone knows the zone in the fridge where you keep leftover meats for lunches. Breads you have left over from dinner can also be used for lunch sandwiches, cutting back on sandwich bread you need to buy. If you want your family to take leftover salad in their lunches, store it in portion-sized plastic containers so it can be grabbed and packed easily.

Repurposing

The trick to being the king or queen of leftovers though is learning to repurpose them—reuse them in sneaky ways so your family doesn't realize they're eating the same thing twice. You'll not only save money, but cut down on kitchen time.

- Use cooked veggies as a topper for garlic bread or in a quiche, frittata, rice, or pasta dish. They're also perfect for soups and stews. Save veggies from a cold veggie plate to be cooked at your next meal, or chop them up and add to a salad.
- Make bread pudding, panzanella, garlic bread, or French toast from leftover bread.
- Mashed potatoes can be made into potato pancakes or as the top layer for shepherd's pie (which can also incorporate leftover meat, veggies, and gravy).
- Whole or sliced potatoes make great hash.
- Rice can be reused in casseroles, turned into rice pilaf, added to soup, and used to make fried rice.
- Extra pasta makes a terrific casserole or can be used in a cold pasta salad.
- Use leftover chicken in a salad, soups, enchiladas, casseroles, or panini. Chop it up to make chicken salad.
- Cut leftover steaks into thin strips and use in beef stroganoff. Put leftover scrambled eggs in fried rice.
- Make meatballs into sloppy joes with some sauce and a little mashing.
- Remains of a pork roast can be shredded and mixed with barbecue sauce for pulled pork sandwiches.

- Too many hamburgers? Save those for sloppy joes or a ground beef casserole.
- Salmon can become salmon patties, which are tasty served on a bun.
- Extra hot dogs make baked beans a full meal.
- Shrimp works well in a salad, or chopped up to make shrimp salad.

Leftover Secrets

When you reheat food, it often dries out. Look for ways to add liquid when you're using it again. Add some more tomato sauce, milk, or broth to a pasta dish or casserole. Soup, stew, and chili need some water to replace that which has evaporated.

If you're working with food to which you can't easily add liquid, look for reheating methods that will help retain moisture. Cover foods completely or wrap in foil if reheating in the oven to keep condensation inside. Steam things like fish or lean chicken to warm them without drying. Use low heat to reuse things like gravies and sauces. They tend to break if you heat over too high a temperature. Stir often. To avoid that reheated flavor and texture with roasts and meats, reheat in the gravy or sauce. The food will stay moist, won't taste old, and will be ready to eat.

Don't put things that need to stay crispy in the microwave. Puff pastry, crusts, fried foods, and things like crunchy potatoes turn to mush when put in the microwave. A time-saving trick is to slightly warm the item first in the micro-wave; then place in a hot oven to crisp it.

SHOP Smart

To use your kitchen wisely, you need to be savvy about how you buy the products you're bringing into it. Organized shoppers use coupons, shop sales, buy in bulk, shop locally, and stay focused when in the store. All of these things can become habits that will allow you to save time and money, buy only what you need, and bring home food and supplies you will actually use.

13

Shopping at Home

Before you head out to go food shopping, take an inventory of what you've already got on your shelves and in your refrigerator to make sure you don't already have some of the items on your list. Money is wasted by buying perishables unnecessarily. If you're keeping a list of what's in your pantry and freezer (see Chapters 6 and 7), consult it to see what you've used up and need. Try to reduce what you need to buy that week by considering what you have at home that you could use up. If you have a garden, go see what's going to be ready in the next week and reduce your purchases in anticipation. Do you have leftovers or something from the freezer you can reheat or repurpose for one meal? Doing so will reduce your shopping bill.

Coupon Craze

How would you like to save $5, $10, or even $50 every time you shop at the supermarket? If this sounds appealing, coupon clipping may be the answer. Searching for and clipping coupons from the newspaper or from advertising circulars can be a time-consuming task, but many people find this to be a relaxing rainy-day or Sunday-afternoon activity.

You can use a binder with clear pockets to sort, categorize, and store your coupons. For example, you may have categories called "Cleaning Products" and "Pet Care Products," and you simply place all related coupons in that category within the same pocket.

An alternative is to use a small file box or small, plastic expandable folder and store your coupons alphabetically, either by product name or brand name. For example, Ivory soap could be filed under "I" for "Ivory" or "S" for "soap," depending on your coupon-filing system.

Another alternative is to use a batch of small envelopes, each marked with a separate coupon category. All the envelopes can be stored together in a larger one so that they are kept together.

Selecting and Storing Coupons

Using coupons can be a fun way to save money, if you're willing to invest the time needed to clip the coupons, bring them to the store, find the right product, and redeem the coupon. As a general rule, clip and store coupons for only those products you already use (or definitely want to try). If you're not careful, your coupon file could easily get cluttered with coupons you have no intention of using.

Before you cut out a coupon, pay attention to the expiration date and the fine print. Also, before clipping it, determine what exactly you need to purchase to redeem the coupon. If you're required to purchase an extra-large container of laundry detergent but you need only a small container, do the math and find out how much the savings will be if you purchase the larger container using the coupon. Some coupons require you to purchase two of one item to get the discount and this can be a problem if you don't have the storage space. Weigh the storage problem against the potential savings. If you can pair the coupon with a rebate or sale, it may be worth having to store the additional item under your bed.

After you clip your coupons, create a written shopping list for yourself. On the list, place a star or some other notation next to the items for which you have a coupon. Next to that item, list the specific name brand and size you need to purchase in order to redeem the coupon.

Finding Coupons

So, where can the best coupons be found? For starters, try the Sunday newspaper and look for inserts and circulars. Look also in the newspaper's weekly food section, which typically appears on Wednesdays. You can also find coupons in general-interest magazines and in women's magazines. Don't forget the Internet. Before you shop, visit the website of the supermarket where you typically shop. Online coupons (which you can print out and redeem) may be offered. If you can match a store coupon with a manufacturer's coupon, you

> Go through your coupon file once a month on or near the first of the month, and cull out all the coupons that expired in the last month.

can save big. There are also websites dedicated specifically to distributing coupons to consumers online. Check out the following:

www.centsoff.com
www.ecoupons.com
www.refundsweepers.com/foodstores.shtml
www.smartsource.net

Coupon Swap

Many supermarkets and libraries offer coupon swap-boxes for consumers. Drop off your unused coupons and grab a few you'll actually use in order to save money. Many supermarkets also have in-store displays that dispense coupons that you can use at checkout. You may also be able to pair up with some friends and cut coupons for each other.

Rebating

Rebates can be a great way to save money as well. You can find them in the coupon section of the newspaper, but they may also be found in store ads, attached to products in the stores, or on manufacturer websites. Some stores offer rebates that accumulate in your store online account all month, and then they send you a check for all of them at the end of the month.

Rebates can be tricky because if you don't follow the terms of the offer exactly, the manufacturer will simply ignore the request. You don't get a chance to correct the problem. It's important to read the offer carefully, including expiration date and the exact requirements. Will they accept a copy of your register receipt or the original only? Do you have to circle the purchase price? Must you include the Universal Product Code (UPC) or other part of the packaging?

When you have the rebate ready to go, make a photocopy of everything you are sending. Write the date on the photocopy so you know when you sent it. If you do not hear from the company in the time indicated on the rebate form, contact them with a copy of the information and ask what has happened to your rebate. Following up like this can bring in big bucks, since most people just mail it in and forget it.

Store Sales

Store sales should be a big part of your planning. Sit down and read the flyer or online notice for the stores in your area. If you have time (most people don't), you might want to plan to go to more than one store to get all the bargains. Check the ad carefully and note items that you use that are on sale. If you don't need the item right now, consider how great the price is. A savings of twenty cents may not be enough incentive for you to bring home another box of dishwashing detergent and have to find a place to keep it.

List It

Consult your meal plan for the week, coupons you want to use that may be expiring, rebates you'd like to send in, and store sales. Write up the list of everything you need. You may want to divide the list into categories to make your shopping easier. If you are shopping on a budget, write the number you can't exceed at the top of the list. You can total mentally as you go, use a calculator as you add things to the cart, or wait till you get to the register to make sure you're under budget.

If you're trying to prevent overspending or if you are sticking to a diet, make it a rule that you will not buy anything that is not on your list.

Download your grocery store's app onto your smartphone. Some stores have apps that allow you to create your list on your phone and have it automatically organized by aisle. These apps are also a lifesaver when you're in the store, think of something you need, but have no idea where it is. Check the app and it will tell you right where to find it. If your store doesn't have one, use an app like Grocery iQ to make a list on your phone organized by aisle.

CSA FYI

Consider joining a CSA (community supported agriculture) for your produce. You buy shares in the CSA for the entire growing season and every week you go and pick up bags and boxes of what the farm has produced that week. Many CSAs offer organic food. Some have programs in which they will drop off the shares at specific locations around the city for easy pickup.

CSAs require you to think differently about how you cook and shop. Get your CSA weekly share before you go to the grocery store or farmers' market. You don't want to go buy lettuce only to find a giant head of lettuce in your CSA bag. Plan your week's meals based on what is in your bag. You may be able to freeze some of the food (or if you're adventurous, can it), but it makes the most sense to get your bag home and then figure out what you can make with it.

Go Organic

The organic food market has grown by leaps and bounds over the past decade. Where organic food was once limited to specialty stores and markets, it's now available almost everywhere. Even Wal-Mart is getting in on the trend, looking to double the number of organic products they sell in the near future. Organic food has even become an important part of restaurants, and food services are being revamped in school cafeterias and corporate lunch counters across the country.

The definition of "organic" varies depending on who is involved in the conversation. Generally, organic refers to the growing, raising, or processing of food without drugs, synthetic chemicals, or hormones, using methods that conserve natural resources and limit the effects on the environment.

Foods meeting the USDA requirements for being organic will have a USDA seal. To obtain the seal, foods must be 95 percent organic. Foods using only organic products and methods may also state "100% organic" on the packaging. A lower level of organic certification is available for foods that are 70 to 95 percent organic. These foods can be labeled as "made with organic ingredients."

According to the Organic Trade Association, the sale of organic foods increased 16 percent in 2005 alone, bringing in $13.8 million in sales. More and more fresh, whole-food, and organic grocery stores are popping up across the United States, and traditional grocers and food producers are starting to take notice.

Believe It—Brand Name Organics

Feeling pressure from growing specialty organic stores, more mainstream grocery stores are including a variety of organic food in their inventories as well. Brands such as Nature's Best and Newman's Own are common in many conventional grocery stores. Many stores have even started their own lines of organic foods. The Kroger Company, the country's largest supermarket, started the Naturally Preferred line in 2002; it now includes more than 275 items. Even large food producers are getting in on the organic options. Kraft Foods now makes USDA-certified organic macaroni and cheese, and their DIGIORNO spinach and garlic thin-crust pizza is made using organic ingredients.

Shopping Savvy

Shopping isn't just about making a list and checking it twice. Be smart about where you buy food and products. Shop for your groceries in a store you would want to go to even if you didn't need to buy food. If you bring home foods that you love from a store that you love, you will be more likely to want to stay home and consume them.

Many cities and towns have wonderful farmers' markets that provide local, seasonal fare. By supporting local farmers, you're able to eat food that you can trust. Because the produce is so fresh, it often looks like edible art, and it lasts longer than food trucked in long distance. You can make the most of your fresh items from the farmers' market by displaying veggies in a large bowl on your table—this functional centerpiece can be as lovely as it is useful. And a morning spent at the farmers' market is a fun and relaxing way to do your own shopping. Don't forget to bring your own bags or baskets to bring your finds home.

Shopping for Other Products

Most people buy more than food at the grocery store. Over-the-counter drugs, paper products, cleaning products, magazines, and health and beauty items often make their way into carts. The grocery store might not be the smartest place to buy these, though.

It takes some sleuthing to find out where best to buy products, but if you have a smartphone, download the app Red Laser, which allows you to scan a barcode and then compare prices at local stores. You might be amazed at some of the price differences for some of these items. Amazon.com also has an app that allows you to check prices on its site, which can often be very low, particularly if you get free shipping.

If you aren't wired for apps, visit discount stores, dollar stores, drugstores, and home stores to check for good prices on nonfood products. Make a note of where you find the best price so you'll remember where to go to get certain items.

Bulking Up

Bulk shopping at stores like Costco, Sam's Club, and other warehouse stores can save lots of money, but it requires you to buy large quantities of items and pay a yearly membership fee. Before joining, walk around the store and note prices on items you commonly use. Do the math to be able to compare the product to the size package you normally buy at the grocery store. Sometimes the savings are huge and sometimes they aren't that impressive when you factor in the yearly fee.

It can be tempting to go overboard at these kinds of stores, because everything seems like such a great deal, but remember you've not only got to find a place to keep the items when you get home, but you've got to make sure you use the food by its expiration dates. You might think your kids like chocolate chip granola bars, but halfway through a box of 100, they may decide they never want to eat another one.

These stores can also entice you to buy something you normally wouldn't, because it's a product you've never seen before. Buying a new item in bulk can be a big mistake because if you don't care for it, you're stuck with it. Some people team up with a friend or relative and shop in bulk together, which allows you to get the discount, but bring home smaller quantities.

Stay Organized at the Store

In addition to planning ahead, how you behave in the store itself has a big impact on how much you spend and what you bring home. Shopping with kids almost always means you will buy additional items, because they will ask for them. You can also be less organized if you've got a screamer in the cart that day because you just can't focus on what you're supposed to be getting in each aisle and you end up making multiple trips around the store, or forgetting things. When you've got an unhappy child along you feel harried in general, which makes you more apt to toss convenience foods in the cart because you cannot conceive of the idea of actually being able to cook from scratch.

Many grocery stores offer free on-site daycare while you shop. Make sure there is an identification system (such as matching bracelets) and an alarm on the entrance door to the children's area. Scope the place out to determine if there are sick children present or if it seems like there are too many kids at once.

Going to the store hungry is also problematic. If you know you're going to hit the store after work or at another time when you're likely to be hungry, bring a healthy snack along to eat in the car before you go. You'll be less likely to splurge and you'll be able to focus better on the task at hand.

Save time by weighing your produce and bulk items yourself if your store has self-serve scales. Remember that anything that has been chopped, sliced, juiced, peeled, washed, cubed, or made into a complete dish is going to end up costing you more than if you handled the whole food yourself and did the work in your own kitchen. Experts recommend focusing on the outside aisles of the store, where you will find fresh produce, meat, and dairy, as the healthiest places to spend most of your store time.

If you're shopping in hot weather, bring an insulated cooler bag along to transport your frozen items.

Checkout Time

Once you've loaded all your items in the cart, your work may seem as if it were over, but there are a few more things you need to pay attention to before you're out of the store. Watch the register as each item is scanned. This is especially important when produce codes are being entered by your checker.

- You know that you bought snap peas, not sweet peas, but he or she might not know the distinction, and there can be a big price difference.
- Keep your eye out for unintentional double scans of items.
- Make sure everything you buy gets put in your bags. Checkers often put fragile or lightweight items aside, meaning to put them on top of heavy items, but then sometimes forget them.
- Ask if your store loyalty card went through.
- Make sure all your coupons scan correctly.
- If you pay by credit card, be sure your checker enters the amount of your purchase as the amount being charged.
- Make sure you get a receipt! Contrary to popular belief, you can return perishable items to the grocery store if you get them home and determine they are out of date, rotten, stale, etc. You can also return nonperishables if you decide you just don't need or want them.

14

On a **PLATE**

Mealtime is a relaxing time when you can enjoy each other's company, the beautiful kitchen you are in, and the meal that has been prepared. A big part of a meal is how the food looks. If something tastes amazing, but is presented in an unattractive way, people are less likely to eat it. Sometimes you work so hard to pull a meal together that presentation is the last thing on your mind. With a few simple tricks, you can make any meal look lovely.

Tabled

Make your meals look attractive by setting a pretty table for each meal. When your family comes to sit down at a table that is orderly and pleasing to the eye, they will be more inclined to stay.

First, completely clear off the table. Take away everything that is not related to the meal. Set a plate in front of each chair that will be used. Don't use plates that are cracked or chipped. Feel free to mix and match dinnerware, as long as you make it look intentional. Use two types of plates and set them every other one, or use all different plates which coordinate. Place the fork on the left and the knife and spoon on the right (knife closest to the plate). Fold or roll the napkin and place it either on the plate or next to the fork. Set the drinking glass above the knife.

When dining in the kitchen, try to straighten up the cooking area before you sit down. Even if you stack pots in the sink or hide them in the oven, it will make the room feel less cluttered and neater.

Always have something in the center of your table, even if it is a houseplant or pretty bowl. Set out the salt and pepper on the table. If you will be placing a hot dish on the table, use a trivet.

If your family needs condiments for the meal, considering placing them in small serving dishes with spoons. It looks so much prettier than plopping bottles of ketchup and mustard on the table.

Serve It Up

There are two ways to serve meals—family-style and individual plates. If there are just two of you for dinner, individual plating is a nice way to go. It reduces the number of dishes and makes the table feel cozier, like you're at a restaurant.

When you serve family-style, place your food in attractive serving bowls and platters. They needn't match your dinnerware. Buy fun pieces at yard sales, thrift shops, and discount stores. Use a basket with a kitchen towel or napkin in it for bread or rolls. Use a serving utensil in each dish. It's okay if they aren't the same pattern as your flatware. Mix and match those.

Get Garnished

Garnishing is the easiest way to make your bowls and plates of food look good enough to eat. When you take two seconds to decorate the food, it transforms it from food into a meal. You don't need to be a restaurant chef to decorate your plates.

Start by seeing what you have in your fridge. Anything leafy and green works as a garnish—parsley, spinach, lettuce, even carrot tops. Any fresh herb looks terrific. Tuck the greenery around the edge of the plate and you have instant panache. Cherry tomatoes, radishes, olives, lemon slices, and lime slices also add to the attractiveness of a plate. Just be sure you put garnishes on that somehow work with the food. Lemon slices wouldn't work with a bowl of coleslaw and lettuce wouldn't go with a bowl of chili.

Think about plating things together. Steaks alone on a platter look pretty boring, but if you put your asparagus next to it, you have something interesting. If you're serving corn and peas, put them next to each other in one big bowl.

Use herbs and spices to dress up your dishes. Sprinkle paprika on top of potato salad, cinnamon on rice pudding, or chopped cilantro on a chicken breast. If you are serving meat with a sauce, place the sauce on the platter or plate first; then top with the meat. Adding height to any dish you serve will make it appealing. Do this by laying the edge of one pork chop over the edge of another, taking some fresh chives or other sprigs of herbs, and leaning them against the food, or crisscrossing your asparagus. Arrange the food in eye-catching ways. For example, if you've made some homemade sweet potato wedges, line them up on the plate uniformly instead of piling them in a bowl.

Easy Entertaining

Even if you're not Martha Stewart, you can enjoy hosting people in your kitchen, and you can put your guests at ease with the relaxed, hospitable atmosphere you provide. When the idea of entertaining fills you with dread, it's time to lower your expectations for yourself. Your own attitude toward the event will permeate the atmosphere, so you want to be as relaxed as possible. Sometimes the only way to be calm before company arrives is to cut back on ceremony and accept your own limitations. You might, for example, serve a fork-only buffet. If guests can only use one type of silverware, you are less likely to spend hours cooking and use multiple dishes. Your kitchen counter is the perfect place to set up a buffet. If you're short on space, put some butcher blocks over your stovetop (as long as it's cool) and sink. This will give you more space to place food.

Have a Plan

Develop one or two meals that are easy for you to make and which you enjoy serving to guests. Keep the things you need on hand so you can pull these quick meals together when you have unexpected guests. You might even consider freezing some dishes you can just pull out and defrost and serve to guests. Casseroles are great for serving guests because you can serve a lot of people from one big dish. These also do double duty as dishes you can keep in your freezer to bring to people in need—those who are ill, have experienced a death in the family, or have just moved into a new home.

Takeout Tips

First of all, there is no law against ordering takeout for guests—just use your own plates to make the meal feel homier. Today most grocery stores sell home-style meals that look just like a delicious home-cooked meal. No one will ever know you didn't make it. You can also bring some fresh flowers in from the garden and use a nice tablecloth or placemats (perhaps with candles?) to make your home feel more welcoming.

Go Potluck

If you feel overwhelmed by the idea of hosting a crowd and feeding them a full meal, by all means, take people up on their offers to contribute food to the gathering—or even let them know up front what you'd like them to bring. Some guests might even want to join you in the kitchen to prepare their dishes. Cooking with others can transform a task that feels like a chore into a joy. Potlucks are a bit of an adventure, because you never know exactly what your guests will come up with—this can be part of the fun, too. Just as all of your guests will bring their own presence into your home for the celebration, so too, they'll have a chance to plan and prepare their own piece of the feast. Keep in mind that potlucks can simplify your life in another way—the guests go home with their own large serving bowls to clean.

The Good Stuff

On special occasions you may pull out your good china. Most people only get it out a few times a year. Since most fine china can go in the dishwasher, why not use it a little more often? Set a fancy table for Sunday dinners once a month. Doing so will make everyone feel special. You'll want to take good care of fine china, though.

Protect your fine, hard-to-replace china from chips and scratches. Buy some felt pads and nestle them in between plates and bowls to act as cushions when you're stacking. Old cloth napkins and even inexpensive coffee filters will do the job, too. And never clean delicate china with harsh abrasives or steel-wool pads. The harm you do may be irreparable. Perhaps your kitchen dining area has built-in storage or a stand-alone storage piece. This storage can be useful if you are intentional about items you place there. Not only can you keep fine china separate from your everyday dishes, but you can also keep part of this storage empty so that you have a place to stow papers and other items when company is coming.

If your cabinet has glass doors, your china will be pretty well protected as you show off the beauty of your pieces. If your fine china will be stored in drawers or closed cabinets, however, you'll want to take steps to protect these expensive and fragile items. Using quilted-vinyl cases for china, for example, will help keep dust away, and at the same time will help prevent chipping and scratching. To prevent chips and scratches while storing china in these padded-vinyl cases, a separate soft-foam protector is placed in between each item. These cases can then be safely stored in a drawer or cabinet.

If a piece of your fine china, crystal, or formal flatware happens to break, chip, or get badly scratched, and your pattern or design has been discontinued, you can find companies that buy and sell discontinued china patterns and other formal dinnerware.

Good Silver

While sterling silver is beautiful, it tarnishes over time. There are many different metal polishes on the market. Some polishes can be corrosive, so take care to follow the manufacturer's instructions.

Keeping your flatware shining is one aspect of the "glory work" involved in making your dining space work. While it can be a headache, it can also be satisfying because the results are almost immediate—polishing your flatware can feel like getting a whole new set for just the cost of the polish.

When washing your fine flatware, use only warm, sudsy water. Carefully rinse away traces of food from the flatware. Avoid using harsh dishwashing detergents that contain chlorides. Also, avoid lemon-scented detergents, which contain acids that may harm the metal. It's also important to hand dry silver, especially knife blades, to avoid spotting and pitting.

Kitchen Linens

You'll want to have a plan for the times you use your linens. They can add a lovely touch to the table, but storing them can be a little tricky. Here are some tips for making your linens work for you.

Before you purchase table linen, be sure to know the exact measurements of your table. Pay attention to the shape of the table on the package—it can be easy to find the perfect table linen that won't actually fit when you get home. A formal tablecloth should hang down from the edge of the tabletop approximately eighteen inches.

Refrain from storing fine table linen in the original plastic packaging. A plastic container or bag will trap moisture and bacteria, which could eventually cause discoloration. Also, don't store your table linens so tightly folded that they crease. Keeping a tightly folded tablecloth in an overcrowded drawer, for example, will damage the fabric over time.

If you're about to invest in an expensive tablecloth, begin your table-linen collection by choosing a classic white linen or classic damask tablecloth, along with a matching set of napkins. You can later expand this collection with a solid-color cloth that matches an accent color in your dinnerware pattern, for example. Another option is to buy one good lace tablecloth, then go to the fabric store and buy an inexpensive length of colored fabric to place underneath it and peek through the lace. Think outside the box for tablecloths. A large U.S. or world map will cover your kitchen table and create a colorful backdrop to your meal. A collection of Sunday comics can also cover your table in a fun way. A funky twin bedspread can do double duty to set your table.

Linens alone will not protect your table. Purchase table pads to go beneath a tablecloth. These pads will greatly extend the life of your table and decrease your own panic when a hot item is set down on the table or a glass of wine spills.

Don't be afraid to wash genuine linen tablecloths and napkins in your washing machine. Just set the washer to delicate and use cool water. Fine linen improves in appearance and feel with every wash. Just as you would with expensive bed linen, iron your table linen while it's still damp, on the back side. This will help prevent any shiny patches from forming. Make sure the iron isn't too hot. When storing fine table linens, always launder and iron (or professionally clean) them properly before putting them into storage.

Placemats

Placemats are an excellent tabletop solution and usually don't require any ironing! Check the care labels on your placemats. Most fabric placemats are machine washable. Those that are not fabric can usually be wiped clean with a damp cloth. Get creative with placemats. A bandana can work as a colorful placemat, as can large pieces of paper colored by your children or wrapping paper cut out with a zigzag scissors.

Don't forget about using a runner in place of a tablecloth or placemats. It's less likely to get dirty and provides a bright swath of color down the center of the table.

For a special occasion, leave a little favor at each place setting, like a small piece of candy, a little flower in a vase, or even a scratch-off lottery ticket.

Napkins and Rings

As with other table linens, there are several affordable and fun ways to create napkins and napkin rings. Men's shirts can be cut down into napkins using zigzag scissors, as can just about any fabric you find at the fabric store. Colorful paper napkins are just as pretty as cloth and require no laundry.

There are so many ways to create your own napkin rings: ribbons, old bent spoons, bangles, Christmas tree ornaments, etc. You can also take any ribbon and tie, glue, or tuck something seasonal or fun onto it or into it (like chestnuts: use a drill to make a hole in them for the ribbon to go through), stick some wildflowers or a fall leaf in it, or tuck a candy bar in it for Valentine's Day, or a feather.

Centerpieces

All eyes are drawn to the center of your table, so use this as an area to dress up the meal. Centerpieces do not have to be expensive flower arrangements; they can be anything pretty, fun, seasonal, or interesting that adds interest to the table. A vase of wildflowers is an easy solution, but there are so many other inexpensive ways to decorate.

Scatter seashells, confetti, streamers, leaves, votive candles, bows, rhinestones, or little shapes cut out of paper across the center of the table. Place a bowl/basket/vase/plate of rocks, shells, candles, sand, driftwood, Christmas ornaments, bark, fake snow, candy hearts, Easter eggs, oranges—almost anything you can think of—on the table. Try to come up with one thing you can just leave on the table for at least a month and not have to think about it.

Appendix A

Web Resources

Now that you've developed a plan for organizing your home, you'll want to home in on the services that will help you to achieve your goals. The following web resources offer information about specific storage solutions and charitable organizations, as well as contact information for professional organizers.

Organizational Consultants

California Closets
www.calclosets.com

Closet Factory
www.closetfactory.com

The National Association of Professional Organizers
www.napo.net

Organization by Design, Inc.
www.dressingwell.com

Storage by Design
www.storagebydesign.com

Companies That Carry Organizational Products

The Container Store
www.containerstore.com

Container World
www.storagesources.com

Frontgate
www.frontgate.com

Ikea
www.ikea-usa.com

Lillian Vernon
www.lillianvernon.com

Lock and Lock
www.LockandLock.com

Organize.com
www.organize.com

The Sharper Image
www.sharperimage.com

Stacks and Stacks
www.stacksandstacks.com

Unique Organizational Products

Brookstone
www.brookstone.com

Restoration Hardware
www.restorationhardware.com

Rubbermaid
www.rubbermaid.com

Shelving Direct
www.shelving-direct.com

Solutions
www.solutionscatalog.com

Kitchen/Dining Products, Services, and Information

Kitchens.com
www.kitchens.com

Kitchen Source
www.kitchensource.com

Kitchenweb
www.kitchenweb.com

Set Your Table: Discontinued Tableware Dealers Directory
www.setyourtable.com

Williams-Sonoma
www.williams-sonoma.com

Safety Products and Information

Fight Bac!
www.fightbac.org

Safety 1st Childcare Products
www.safety1st.com

United States Consumer Product Safety Commission
www.cpsc.gov

Cleaning Supplies and Cleaning Information

Clean Report
www.cleanreport.com

Seventh Generation
www.seventhgeneration.com

House-Cleaning Tips
www.housecleaning-tips.com/cleaning-a-kitchen.html

Refrigeration and Food Safety

USDA Refrigeration Guide
www.fsis.usda.gov/factsheets/ refrigeration_&_food_safety/index.asp

USDA Freezing Guide
www.fsis.usda.gov/factsheets/focus_on_ freezing/index.asp

Appendix B

Helpful Books

The author wishes gratefully to acknowledge the work of the following authors. These books provided inspiration during the process of writing and researching this book. Should you wish to further explore any of the ideas you've read about in these pages, these resources are a great place to start. They explore a variety of aspects related to homemaking, such as aesthetics, organization, cleaning, and productivity issues.

Anderson, Candace, with Nicole Cormier. *The Everything® Freezer Meals Cookbook* (Avon, MA: F+W Media, Inc., 2010). This book is packed with recipes you can make and freeze.

Cilley, Marla. *Sink Reflections* (New York: Bantam Dell, 2002). This extremely down-to-earth and practical book is written by the FlyLady in an accessible style and offers many helpful hints for getting your home (and life) in order.

Hollender, Jeffrey, Geoff Davis, and Meika Hollender. *Naturally Clean: The Seventh Generation Guide to Safe & Healthy, Non-Toxic Cleaning* (British Columbia: New Society Publishers, 2006). This book offers an in-depth look at the hazards associated with household cleaners and indoor air pollution.

Lawrence, Robyn Griggs. *The Wabi-Sabi House: The Japanese Art of Imperfect Beauty* (New York: Clarkson Potter, 2004). This book offers an insightful introduction to the concept of *wabi-sabi*. It is a pleasure to read and is illustrated with beautiful photographs.

Moran, Victoria. *Shelter for the Spirit: Create Your Own Haven in a Hectic World* (New York: HarperCollins, 1998). This book is a personal, reflective guide to creating a home that is both aesthetically pleasing and comforting to your soul.

Morgenstern, Julie. *Organizing from the Inside Out: The Foolproof System for Organizing Your Home, Your Office and Your Life*, 2nd ed. (New York: Henry Holt & Co., 2004). Julie Morgenstern draws from years of experience as a professional organizer, distilling her wisdom into this practical, easy-to-read guide to getting your home in order.

St. James, Elaine. *Simplify Your Life: 100 Ways to Slow Down and Enjoy the Things That Really Matter* (New York: Hyperion, 1994). This quick read offers useful tips for streamlining your home and life, improving your health, and learning to enjoy life's simplest joys.

Index

bout the Author

Sember is the author of *The Parchment Paper Cookbook* (F+W Media, 011) and *The Muffin Tin Cookbook* (F+W Media, Inc., 2012). She is the of the blog *www.MarthaAndMe.net*, where she informally apprenticed to Martha Stewart for a year and reorganized her entire kitchen and other f her home, based on Martha's advice. Sember also blogs about cook- www.NoPotCooking.com.

e has written for over 200 magazines about food, family, and organiz- well as over thirty books about many other topics. She is a member of rnational Association of Culinary Professionals, the American Society of ists and Authors, is the recipient of a Mothers at Home Media Award and Ben Franklin Award finalist. Her website is *www.brettesember.com*.

About the Author

Brette Sember is the author of *The Parchment Paper Cookbook* (F+W Media, Inc., 2011) and *The Muffin Tin Cookbook* (F+W Media, Inc., 2012). She is the owner of the blog *www.MarthaAndMe.net*, where she informally apprenticed herself to Martha Stewart for a year and reorganized her entire kitchen and other areas of her home, based on Martha's advice. Sember also blogs about cooking at *www.NoPotCooking.com*.

She has written for over 200 magazines about food, family, and organizing, as well as over thirty books about many other topics. She is a member of the International Association of Culinary Professionals, the American Society of Journalists and Authors, is the recipient of a Mothers at Home Media Award and was a Ben Franklin Award finalist. Her website is *www.brettesember.com*.